28 MOCK TEST SERIES for Olympiad

English	Mathematics
Science	General Knowledge
Cyber	Logical Reasoning

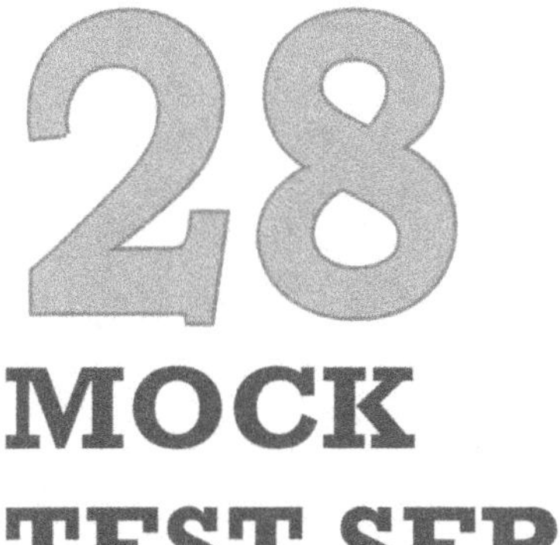

1

Class

Comprehensive MCQ with detailed solutions covering all the Olympiad Exams.

- **Corporate Office :** 45, 2nd Floor, Maharishi Dayanand Marg, Corner Market, Malviya Nagar, New Delhi-110017
  Tel. : 011-49842349 / 49842350

Typeset by Disha DTP Team

Printed at Repro Knowledgecast Limited, Thane

For further information about the books from DISHA,

Log on to **www.dishapublication.com** or email to **info@dishapublication.com**

CONTENTS

English

Mathematics

Science

General Knowledge

Logical Reasoning

Cyber

ENGLISH MOCK TEST 1-5

OLYMPIAD
Mock Test 1 −

Name : ___________

Number of Questions : 35

There is no negative marking in the test.

Max. Marks : 35

Time : 2 Hours

Section I
Word and Structure Knowledge

Directions (Qs. 1 to 3): Identify the odd one out.

1. (a) Starfish   (b) Octopus

   (c) Shark   (d) Cow

2. (a) Computer   (b) Mouse

   (c) Cat   (d) Monitor

3. (a) Fork   (b) Spoon

   (c) Plate   (d) Pencil

Directions (Qs. 4 to 6): Look at the picture and identify the correct word.

4. 

   (a) Shirt   (b) Coat

   (c) Tie   (d) Trousers

5.

   (a) Television

   (b) Washing Machine

   (c) Refrigerator

   (d) Computer

Space for Rough Work

6.

(a) Rain

(b) Cloud

(c) Umbrella

(d) Sky

Directions (Qs. 7 & 8): Identify the picture and choose the correct spelling.

7.

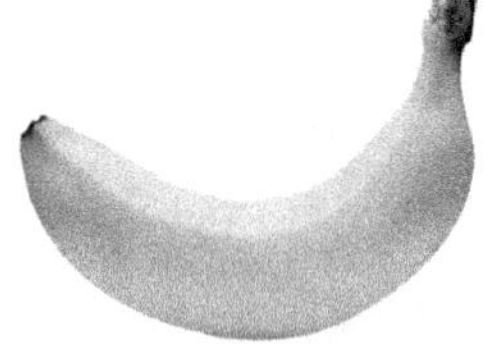

(a) Bnana

(b) Banana

(c) Bannana

(d) Bananaa

8.

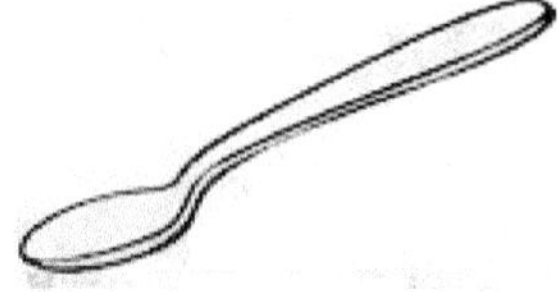

(a) Spoon   (b) Spun

(c) Spoen   (d) Spin

Directions (Qs. 9 & 10): Choose a meaningful word from the given options.

9. (a) Alts   (b) Salt

    (c) Tals   (d) Lats

10. (a) Potato   (b) Patoto

     (c) Pattoo   (d) Potota

Directions (Qs. 11 to 18): Choose the right word.

11. The opposite of **ladies** is ________.

    (a) men   (b) gentlemen

    (c) boys   (d) women

12. The opposite of **lion** is _________.

    (a) lioness   (b) tigress

    (c) queen   (d) cat

13. The young one of a **deer** is ______.

    (a) foal   (b) fawn

    (c) cub   (d) colt

14. The young one of a **frog** is _______.

    (a) kitten   (b) puppy

    (c) spiderling   (d) tadpole

15. He ______there everyday.

    (a) go

    (b) goes

    (c) going

    (d) none of these

16. The ______were howling.

    (a) wolf   (b) wolves

    (c) wolfes   (d) wolfs

17. I have two pencil ________.

    (a) boxs   (b) box

    (c) boxes   (d) boxies

18. The ___________ are in the ground.

    (a) sheeps   (b) sheepies

    (c) sheep   (d) sheepz

Directions (Qs. 19 to 21): Choose the opposite.

19. Sleep – _________

    (a) Awake   (b) Drowsy

    (c) Play   (d) Dance

Space for Rough Work

20. Difficult – _______________

   (a) Tough   (b) Easy

   (c) Top   (d) Deep

21. Rough – ___________

   (a) Hard   (b) Soft

   (c) Smooth   (d) Light

Section II
Comprehension

Directions (Qs. 22 to 25) : Look at the picture and choose the right answer.

22. My name is Riya. I'm a _______.

   (a) doctor   (b) nurse

   (c) teacher   (d) pilot

23. I ___________.

   (a) give medicines

   (b) teach children

   (c) drive an aeroplane

   (d) sweep floors

24. I go to________.

   (a) hotel   (b) hospital

   (c) school   (d) airport

25. I write on the blackboard with a ____.

   (a) pen   (b) pencil

   (c) chalk   (d) crayon

———————— Space for Rough Work ————————

Directions (Qs. 26 to 28): Read the passage and complete the sentences that follow.

Ramu, the elephant, was a very kind elephant. While walking, it used to be very careful about stepping on the ants. One day, one rabbit came to it for help. Ramu was very pleased to help the rabbit. The rabbit wanted Ramu to go with him to scare off the lion. Ramu had never seen the lion before. So, Ramu agreed to go with the rabbit. When they reached near the den of the lion, Ramu heard the lion's roar. Hearing the roar, Ramu got scared. But since it had promised the rabbit to help, it stayed on. The moment the lion came out and roared, Ramu ran away with all its might.

26. Ramu was a _______ elephant.

   (a) kind   (b) ferocious

   (c) happy   (d) sad

27. A _______ came to Ramu for help.

   (a) lion   (b) monkey

   (c) mouse   (d) rabbit

28. After seeing lion, Ramu _______.

   (a) fought with it

   (b) ran away

   (c) had an argument

   (d) roared

—————————— *Space for Rough Work* ——————————

Section III
Spoken and Written Expressions

Directions (Qs. 29 to 35): Choose the most appropriate option to fill the blanks.

29. Happy birthday to you.

____

(a) Why did you say that?

(b) Thank you.

(c) Sure, thanks.

(d) No, thanks.

30. Hello, I am Tim.

____

(a) I am 7 years old.

(b) He is not my friend.

(c) He likes to eat chocolates.

(d) Yes, I like my dog Frazy.

31. Is he your friend?

____

(a) No, I am his cousin.

(b) No, he is my cousin.

(c) What kind of a question is this?

(d) He didn't like your house.

32. Have you been to Mussoorie?

____

(a) Yes, it's a lovely place.

(b) Why should I go there?

(c) No, Shimla is a better place.

(d) I did not get time.

———————— Space for Rough Work ————————

33. Hello, how are you?

____

   (a)   No, I am not so good.

   (b)   I am fine, how about you?

   (c)   What a funny question!

   (d)   Yes, thank you.

34. I got hurt on my toe.

____

   (a)   That's great news.

   (b)   Oh! Did you take any medicine?

   (c)   That's a terrible thing.

   (d)   Let's go for a walk now.

35. Teacher: Have you done your homework?

Student:___________________________

   (a)   I did not, as there was no need to do it.

   (b)   Yes, Ma'am.

   (c)   No, I thought playing was better.

   (d)   I can do it tomorrow.

OLYMPIAD
Mock Test 2

Name : __________

Number of Questions : 35

Max. Marks : 35

Time : 2 Hours

There is no negative marking in the test.

Section I
Word and Structure Knowledge

Directions (Qs. 1 to 4): Look at the picture and choose the correct word.

1.

(a) Vase   (b) Glass

(c) Pot   (d) Bottle

2. 

(a) Chair   (b) Table

(c) Stool   (d) Sofa

3. 

(a) Computer   (b) Television

(c) Laptop   (d) Microwave

4. 

(a) Bus   (b) Car

(c) Truck   (d Van

Directions (Qs. 5 to 7): Find the odd one out.

5. (a) Man   (b) Woman

(c) Boy   (d) Lion

———— Space for Rough Work ————

6. (a) North   (b) South

   (c) West   (d) Town

7. (a) Venus   (b) Earth

   (c) Sun   (d) Mars

Directions (Qs. 8 to 10): Choose the right word that goes with the first one.

8. Bread and ______

   (a) Butter   (b) Cheese

   (c) Jam   (d) Egg

9. Sun and ______

   (a) Stars   (b) Moon

   (c) Sky   (d) Clouds

10. Give and ______

   (a) Go   (b) Come

   (c) Forget   (d) Take

Directions (Qs. 11 to 14): Choose the right word.

11. You bite with your____________.

   (a) nails   (b) teeth

   (c) hands   (d) knife

12. You write with a _________.

   (a) pen   (b) eraser

   (c) pencil box   (d) notebook

13. You smell with your___________.

   (a) eyes   (b) nose

   (c) skin   (d) tongue

14. You watch a ______.

   (a) movie   (b) pen

   (c) book   (d) time

———————————— *Space for Rough Work* ————————————

Directions (Qs. 15 to 18): Choose the word which does not rhyme with the given word.

15. Deer

    (a) Dare   (b) Dear

    (c) Fear   (d) Sheer

16. Match

    (a) Catch   (b) Latch

    (c) Batch   (d) Torch

17. Ball

    (a) Call   (b) Hall

    (c) Shall   (d) Tall

18. Hair

    (a) Fair   (b) Chair

    (c) Pair   (d) Sir

Section II

Comprehension

Directions (Qs. 19 to 22): Look at the picture and answer the questions that follow.

19. The girl is playing with a________.

    (a) doll   (b) slide

    (c) swing   (d) kite

20. The first girl at upper left corner is ______

    (a) riding a bicycle.

    (b) swinging on swings.

    (c) playing with a racquet.

    (d) playing with a football.

Space for Rough Work

21. The boy at upper right corner is

    ____

(a) listening to music.

(b) playing with football.

(c) running on track.

(d) playing with the swings.

22. The girl at bottom right corner is_________

(a) swinging.

(b) skipping the rope.

(c) playing with a doll.

(d) riding on a bicycle.

Directions (Qs. 23 to 27): Read the poem and answer the questions.

I Saw a Rainbow

I saw a rainbow,

It had so many colours,

I wonder how?

It seem so wondrous,

In beauty and

I want to touch you,

I want to reach you,

I want all the colours you have

Violet, Indigo, Blue, Green, Yellow,

Orange and Red.

23. What did the author see?

(a) Sky   (b) Rainbow

(c) Stars   (d) Moon

24. The author found it to be_________.

(a) wonderful (b) beautiful

(c) bright   (d) colourful

25. How many colours does the rainbow have?

(a) Six   (b) Seven

(c) One   (d) Twelve

_________________ *Space for Rough Work* _________________

26. One colour that is not there in a rainbow is __________.

    (a) green   (b) black

    (c) red   (d) yellow

27. The author wants to _______

    (a) bring the rainbow down.

    (b) reach and touch the rainbow.

    (c) become rainbow.

    (d) touch the stars.

Section III

Spoken and Written Expression

Directions (Qs. 28 to 33): Choose the the most appropriate option to fill the blanks.

28. Hello! Is it 55998877?

    ____

    (a) Yes, I am Seema.

    (b) No, you are wrong.

    (c) Yes, may I know who is calling?

    (d) No, it's my number.

29. Shopkeeper: May I help you?

    Customer: _____________________

    (a) Yes, do you have double-door fridges?

    (b) No, it's okay.

    (c) Is it tough to help me?

    (d) You better stay out.

30. Receptionist at a hotel: Yes, Sir! How may I help you?

    Customer: _____________________

    (a) I am helpless.

    (b) You better look your way.

    (c) Yes, I was looking for a room.

    (d) I cannot be helped.

Space for Rough Work

31. Has your mom allowed you to go out?

____

   (a) I don't need to ask her.

   (b) Yes, but she has told me to come early.

   (c) I don't want to go.

   (d) Why should I tell you?

32. Do you like chocolates?

____

   (a) Yes, I really like them.

   (b) No, they are so bad.

   (c) Yes, I like sweets.

   (d) No, chips are better.

33. Hello Tanya! What are you doing?

Tanya: _______________________________

   (a) Why should I tell you?

   (b) My mother is cooking food.

   (c) I cannot say.

   (d) I was sleeping.

34. Doctor: How are you?

Patient: _______________________________

   (a) Who are you to ask me this?

   (b) Better, thanks!

   (c) That was your duty.

   (d) I am not going to come.

35. Teacher: Why didn't you complete your work?

Student: _______________________________

   (a) I did not feel like.

   (b) My mom told me not to do it.

   (c) Ma'am! I was not well.

   (d) My brother had gone out.

Space for Rough Work

OLYMPIAD
Mock Test ③ ▬

Name : ___________

Number of Questions : 40

There is no negative marking in the test.

Max. Marks : 40

Time : 2 Hours

Section I
Word and Structure Knowledge

Directions (Qs. 1 to 5): Look at the picture and choose the correct word.

1. 

   (a) Cone   (b) Top

   (c) Bow   (d) Swing

2. 

   (a) Leaf   (b) Flower

   (c) Bud   (d) Plant

3. 

   (a) Scooter   (b) Bicycle

   (c) Motorcycle   (d) Car

4. 

   (a) Boat   (b) Submarine

   (c) Ship   (d Car

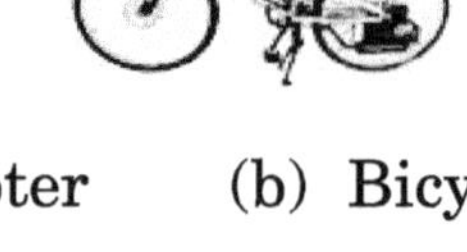

———— Space for Rough Work ————

Directions (Qs. 5 to 8): Choose the odd one out.

5. (a) Watermelon

   (b) Orange

   (c) Apple

   (d) Cabbage

6. (a) Newspaper (b) Book

   (c) Chocolate (d) Comics

7. (a) Teacher (b) Principal

   (c) Student (d) Classroom

8. (a) Den (b) Kennel

   (c) Cub (d) Nest

Directions (Qs. 9 to 12): Choose a meaningful word from the given options.

9. (a) Lino (b) Lion

   (c) Noil (d) Oinl

10. (a) Fethar (b) Father

    (c) Ferath (d) Fathre

11. (a) Kinfe (b) Knefi

    (c) Knife (d) Kifne

12. (a) Fridge (b) Frigde

    (c) Fredgi (d) Firgde

Directions (Qs. 13 & 14): Choose the right word.

13. A group of leopards is called____.

    (a) pride (b) leap

    (c) litter (d) colony

14. A kangaroo __________________.

    (a) barks (b) chortles

    (c) pipes (d) roars

Space for Rough Work

Section II
Reading

Directions (Qs. 15 to 18): Read the poem and answer the questions that follow.

My Mom is the Greatest Mom

My mom is the greatest Mom.

I love her very much.

She's there for me,

Every time I need her,

She cooks great food,

She's never in foul mood

It would not have been so easy,

As it is now,

She stands by me when I need her,

She is indeed the greatest mom.

15. My mom is the __________ mom.

(a) greatest   (b) best

(c) happiest   (d) nice

16. She is there for me__________

(a) when I want to go out.

(b) whenever I need her.

(c) when she is cooking.

(d) when I want to sleep.

17. She cooks__________________.

(a) tasty food

(b) chinese food

(c) indian food

(d) healthy food

18. When is she in foul mood?

(a) When I don't listen to her.

(b) When she wants to go out.

(c) She is never in a foul mood.

(d) When she is cooking.

Space for Rough Work

Directions (Qs. 19 to 22): Look at the picture and answer the questions that follow.

19. My name is Lona. I am a ________.
    (a) tiger   (b) lion

    (c) leopard   (d) cat

20. I stay in a ___________________.

    (a) kennel   (b) den

    (c) shed   (d) pigsty

21. My young one is called _________.

    (a) cub   (b) puppy

    (c) kitten   (d) fawn

22. My group is called ____________.

    (a) leap   (b) pride

    (c) litter   (d) mob

Directions (Qs. 23 to 26): Look at the picture and select the right word.

23. This is a scene of a ____________.

    (a) jungle   (b) town

    (c) village   (d) school

Space for Rough Work

24. Which of the following is not shown in the picture?

 (a) Bird   (b) Deer

 (c) Squirrel   (d) Zebra

25. The animals are_______________.

 (a) running

 (b) drinking water

 (c) fighting

 (d) singing

26. The birds are__________________.

 (a) running

 (b) flying

 (c) walking

 (d) eating food

Section III
Spoken and Written Expression

Directions (Qs. 27 to 32): Choose the most appropriate option to fill the blanks.

27. Shreya: Your house is so beautiful!

 Manoj: _____________________

 (a)   No, it is not that big.

 (b)   Thanks.

 (c)   Sure, I will try.

 (d)   Yes, it has to be.

28. You hurt my toe.

 ____

 (a)   I'm so sorry.

 (b)   Which one?

 (c)   Really?

 (d)   Are you joking?

Space for Rough Work

29. Harris: Can you click my photograph?

Nancy: _______________________

(a) What's that?

(b) I don't have time.

(c) Yes sure.

(d) I can't.

30. Doctor: How are you now?

Patient: _______________________

(a) Much better.

(b) What have you done?

(c) Not great!

(d) Please, can you keep silence?

31. Tomorrow is Mother's day.

____

(a) We are planning a party for mom.

(b) My mom is a great cook.

(c) My mom will make cake for us.

(d) My mom does not like to play cricket.

32. Tomorrow is my birthday, will you come?

____

(a) I like birthdays.

(b) I want to wear a dress.

(c) I don't like parties.

(d) Sure, I will come.

Space for Rough Work

Section IV

Achievers Section

Directions (Qs. 33 & 34): Choose the right answer.

33. A group of owls is called a______.

    (a) owlet   (b) parliament

    (c) leap   (d) shoal

34. We must __________our elders.

    (a) respect

    (b) respecting

    (c) respectful

    (d) most respectful

Directions (Qs. 35 & 36): Choose the option that correctly combines given sentences.

35. I have to reach early. I will be late.

    (a) I have to reach early but I will be late.

    (b) I have to reach early or I will be late.

    (c) I have to reach early because I will be late.

    (d) I have to reach early when I will be late.

36. I wanted to go out and play. I could not go.

    (a) I wanted to go out and play when I could not go.

    (b) I wanted to go out and play because I could not go.

    (c) I wanted to go out and play but I could not go.

    (d) I wanted to go out and play or I could not go.

Directions (Qs. 37 & 38): Choose the right answer.

37. I am round and bright, hot and yellow. When I come, I spread light.

    (a) Bulb   (b) Light

    (c) Sun   (d) Fan

38. I have strips on my body that are black and white in colour. I love grass.

(a) Deer (b) Zebra

(c) Giraffe (d) Goat

Directions (Qs. 39 & 40): Choose the correct sentence.

39. (a) George Washington has the President of USA.

(b) George Washington is the president of USA.

(c) George Washington are the President of USA.

(d) George Washington was the president of USA.

40. (a) Tomorrow was Tuesday.

(b) Tomorrow has Tuesday.

(c) Tomorrow is Tuesday.

(d) Tomorrow can Tuesday.

Space for Rough Work

OLYMPIAD
Mock Test 4

Name : __________
Number of Questions : 40

Max. Marks : 40
Time : 2 Hours

There is no negative marking in the test.

Section I
Word and Structure Knowledge

Directions (Qs. 1 to 4): Look at the picture and choose the correct word.

1. 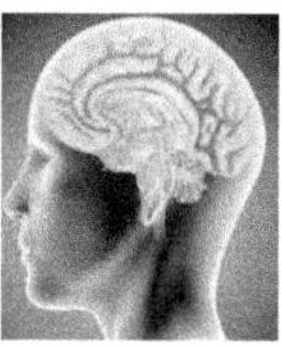

(a) Brain   (b) Heart
(c) Lung   (d) Kidney

2. 

(a) Lollypop   (b) Balloons
(c) Toffees   (d) Streamers

3. 

(a) Policeman   (b) Fireman
(c) Engineer   (d) Chef

4. 

(a) Deer   (b) Donkey
(c) Yak   (d) Jaguar

———— Space for Rough Work ————

Directions (Qs. 5 to 8): Choose the correct word that goes with the first one.

5. You play cricket with a __________.

   (a) bat   (b) wicket

   (c) stick   (d) pad

6. We must never make war but make________.

   (a) peace   (b) piece

   (c) fight   (d) hate

7. Soap and __________

   (a) Water   (b) Bath

   (c) Toilet   (d) Hand

8. In and________

   (a) Inside   (b) Out

   (c) Near   (d) Far

Directions (Qs. 9 to 12): Choose the right answer.

9. I, Seema and Dinesh went by car. ______ enjoyed a lot.

   (a) We   (b) They

   (c) Us   (d) You

10. Mr. Shaan is a teacher. ____ teaches in a school.

   (a) He   (b) She

   (c) You   (d) It

11. Mother: Get ready, quickly! ________ are getting late.

   (a) You   (b) They

   (c) Us   (d) I

12. I saw ____ owl on the tree.

   (a) a   (b) an

   (c) the   (d) none of these

Space for Rough Work

Directions (Qs. 13 & 14): Look at the picture and choose the right answer.

Directions (Qs. 15): Look at the picture and choose the right answer.

13. The man is hiding ___ the sofa.

    (a) above   (b) on

    (c) behind   (d) up

14. There is a wall ___the man.

    (a) in front of (b) behind

    (c) above   (d) under

15. The two boys are fighting ______ each other.

    (a) on   (b) with

    (c) between (d) among

Directions (Qs. 16 to 20): Choose the correct pronoun.

16. He did not want to play with us.

    (a) He   (b) Did

    (c) Not   (d) Play

17. His mother was cooking food when I went there.

    (a) His   (b) Mother

    (c) Was   (d) Cooking

18. You have bad cold. You are sneezing too much.

    (a) You   (b) Bad

    (c) Cold   (d) Sneezing

Directions (Qs. 19 & 20): Choose the most appropriate word to fill the blanks.

19. He wanted to swim in the _______.

    (a) rain   (b) pool

    (c) farm   (d) village

20. When you are crying, you are _________.

    (a) beautiful   (b) sad

    (c) ugly   (d) happy

Directions (Qs. 21 to 25): Find the odd one out.

21. (a) Table   (b) Chair

    (c) Almirah   (d) Kitchen

22. (a) Train   (b) Bus

    (c) Car   (d) Ship

23. (a) Monday   (b) Saturday

    (c) February   (d) Tuesday

24. (a) Apple   (b) Cabbage

    (c) Pear   (d) Pomegranate

25. (a) Crocodile   (b) Fish

    (c) Tortoise   (d) Horse

Space for Rough Work

Section II
Reading

Directions (Qs. 26 to 28): Read the story and answer the questions that follow.

DONKEY'S DAY OUT

Ramu was the name of a donkey. It used to work for a washerman. The washerman used to make it carry a lot of load. Ramu did not like carrying so much load on its back. One day when the washerman was fast asleep in the night, it decided to wander out. It was the first time that it was out in the dark. It came out and started to wander in the moonlight. It kept on wandering. Suddenly it realised that it had gone too far. Now Ramu did not know the way back home. It was scared. It began to bray. The moment it started braying , the washerman heard it. He was amazed as to how the donkey was out!

26. Who was Ramu?

    (a) A washerman

    (b) A cobbler

    (c) A Donkey

    (d) An elephant

27. When did the donkey decide to go out?

    (a) In the morning

    (b) In the afternoon

    (c) In the evening

    (d) In the night

28. When donkey saw itself alone, it began to________.

    (a) neigh   (b) laugh

    (c) bray   (d) bark

—————————— *Space for Rough Work* ——————————

Section III

Spoken and Written Expression

Directions (Qs. 29 to 34): Choose the most appropriate option to fill the blanks.

29. Is this your bicycle?

____

(a) No, it's not my house.

(b) Yes, it's mine.

(c) Do you think so?

(d) My dad got it for me.

30. Is the doctor in?

____

(a) No, he left early today.

(b) Yes, I wanted to go with him.

(c) I can't say.

(d) He is giving medicines.

31. Are you going to the temple?

____

(a) Yes, I am going home.

(b) Yes, I am going there.

(c) Yes, I am going out.

(d) Yes, he is also going.

32. This is my house.

____

(a) Oh, really!

(b) It doesn't seem so.

(c) You have a wonderful house.

(d) My dad told me that.

33. Have you finished your work?

_______________________________ .

(a) Thanks for telling me that.

(b) No, I am still doing it.

(c) No, but it's tough.

(d) I don't want to do it.

——— Space for Rough Work ———

34. Ram: Who is he?

    Farhaan: ______________________

    (a) You don't know?

    (b) He is my friend.

    (c) He is no one.

    (d) He has taken my car.

35. My car broke down.

    ____

    (a) Oh, really!

    (b) That's a great news.

    (c) Oh, that's sad.

    (d) Nothing to worry.

Section IV

Achievers Section

Directions (Qs. 36 & 37): Choose the correct word.

36. I am on your head. I make you look beautiful. You can't count me.

    (a) Ears   (b) Hair

    (c) Eyes   (d) Brain

37. I am a joint between your foot and leg.

    (a) Knee   (b) Elbow

    (c) Ankle   (d) Toe

Directions (Qs. 38 to 40): Choose the correct sentence.

38. _______________________________

(a) Mahatma Gandhi is a father of nation.

(b) Mahatma Gandhi is an Father of the nation.

(c) Mahatma Gandhi is the Father of the Nation.

(d) Mahatma Gandhi is your father of the nation.

39. _______________________________

(a) Jack and jill went up the hill.

(b) Jack and Jill went up the hill.

(c) Jack and Jill went up the hill.

(d) Jack and Jill went up the Hill.

40. _______________________________

(a) 2nd October had Gandhi Jayanti.

(b) 2nd October is could Gandhi Jayanti.

(c) 2nd October have Gandhi Jayanti.

(d) 2nd October is Gandhi Jayanti.

Space for Rough Work

OLYMPIAD
Mock Test 5

Name : ___________

Number of Questions : 35

Max. Marks : 35

Time : 2 Hours

There is no negative marking in the test.

Section I
Word and Structure Knowledge

Directions (Qs. 1 to 4): Look at the picture and choose the correct word.

1. 

   (a) Muskmelon
   (b) Strawberry
   (c) Watermelon
   (d) Cherries

2. 

   (a) Tree

   (b) Shrub

   (c) Plant

   (d) Creeper

3. 

   (a) Cabbage

   (b) Spinach

   (c) Cauliflower

   (d) Carrot

Space for Rough Work

4.

(a) Lotus

(b) Rose

(c) Sunflower

(d) Lily

5.

(a) Eyes

(b) Ears

(c) Nose

(d) Chin

Directions (Qs. 6 to 10): Choose the correct word.

6. (a) Togather   (b) Together

    (c) Tegather   (d) Tegethor

7. (a) Crocodile   (b) Cocrodile

    (c) Corcodile   (d) Circodole

8. (a) Doctor   (b) Docter

    (c) Dector   (d) Dorcot

Directions (Qs. 9 & 10): Look at the picture and answer the questions that follow.

9. I am a __________.

    (a) postman

    (b) policeman

    (c) doctor

    (d) nurse

10. My work is to __________.

    (a) catch thieves

    (b) give medicines

    (c) deliver letters

    (d) mend your shoes

Directions (Qs. 11 to 15): Choose the word that does not belong to the list.

11. Wild animals

  (a) Lion   (b) Snake

  (c) Dog   (d) Elephant

12. Vegetables

  (a) Spinach   (b) Cabbage

  (c) Carrot   (d) Muskmelon

13. Hospital

  (a) Doctor   (b) Soldier

  (c) Patient   (d) Nurse

14. Post Office

  (a) Letter   (b) Parcel

  (c) Student   (d) Postman

15. School

  (a) Teacher   (b) Students

  (c) Principal   (d) Deer

Section II

Reading

Directions (Qs. 16 to 20): Read the following information and answer the questions that follow.

Hello Friends!

Harshit will be celebrating his 8th birthday on 4th February, 2013.

Timings are from 4:30 p.m. to 7: 30 p.m.

Venue: 134, Golf View Apartments, Dadar

You are cordially invited.

For any help, call V. M. Punj. Mobile No. is 9868565537.

16. What is this?

  (a) An invitation to a birthday

  (b) A ticket

  (c) A pass

  (d) An admit card

Space for Rough Work

17. Whose birthday is it?

   (a) Harshit   (b) Abhinav's

   (c) Harris's   (d) Bala's

18. When is the birthday?

   (a) In the morning.

   (b) In the evening.

   (c) In the midnight.

   (d) In the afternoon.

19. Where is the birthday being celebrated?

   (a) At the pool side

   (b) At home

   (c) At the restaurant

   (d) In a farmhouse

20. In case you want to ask the way, whom would you call?

   (a) Harshit

   (b) U.M. Punj

   (c) His neighbour

   (d) His friends

Directions (Qs. 21 to 24): Read the passage and answer the questions that follow.

HEALTHY FOOD

We all must eat healthy food. Healthy food consists of fruit and vegetables. Healthy food makes us strong. It also does not make you fat. Fruit and vegetables keep the diseases away from us. You must have heard the proverb, 'An apple a day, keeps the doctor away'. It applies to all seasonal fruit. Milk and curd make your bones and teeth strong. Healthy food makes your skin glow.

21. Which proverb about apples has been used in the passage?

    (a) 'An apple a day, keeps the doctor away'.

    (b) 'Don't upset the apple cart'.

    (c) 'The old monkey gets the apple'.

    (d) 'A bad tree does not yeild good apples'.

22. Healthy food consists of _________.

    (a) burgers and pizzas

    (b) fruit and vegetables

    (c) water and air

    (d) bread and butter

23. Milk and curd make your______ strong.

    (a) eyes   (b) bones and teeth

    (c) ears   (d) muscles

24. Healthy food keeps ________ away from us.

    (a) neighbours (b) teachers

    (c) diseases   (d) enemies

Section III
Spoken and Written Expression

Directions (Qs. 25 to 28): Choose the best reply to complete each conversation.

25. Dev: I'm going to the museum tomorrow.

    Ved: ____________________________

    (a) Sorry, I can't come with you.

    (b) Sure, you can go.

    (c) Yes, thank you.

    (d) Great! Have fun.

26. Lata: I am going to the market, you want to come?

Sneha: _________________________

(a) Go away.

(b) That's not a good idea.

(c) I want to, but I have some work at home.

(d) It sounds funny.

27. Amit: We are going to the park to play football. Do you want to come?

Sumit: _________________________

(a) I don't want to play football.

(b) Go away.

(c) That's very boring.

(d) I am not good at cricket.

28. Father: Give it back to him, that's not your ball.

Son: _________________________

(a) I can't.

(b) Sure, dad.

(c) He has to snatch it from me.

(d) This is my ball.

Directions (Qs. 29 to 32): Choose the correct sentence.

29. (a) New Delhi is the capital of India.

(b) New Delhi in the capital of India.

(c) New Delhi of the capital of India.

(d) New Delhi at the capital of India.

30. (a) What do he say?

(b) What did he say?

(c) What he say?

(d) What does he says?

31. (a) His sister is stay in Paris.

(b) His sister stay in Paris

(c) His sister staying in Paris.

(d) His sister stays in Paris.

Directions (Qs. 32 & 33): Choose the best option to join the two sentences.

32. I like milk. It should be cold.
    (a) I like milk and it should be cold.

    (b) I like milk as it should be cold.

    (c) I like milk because it should be cold.

    (d) I like milk but it should be cold.

33. I couldn't come. I was not well.
    (a) I couldn't come because I was not well.

    (b) I couldn't come so I was not well.

(c) I couldn't come when I was not well.

(d) I couldn't come but I was not well.

Section IV
Achievers Section

Directions (Qs. 34 & 35): Choose the right answer.

34. A nightingale ____________.

(a) sings

(b) barks

(c) chortles

(d) chatters

35. Shreya did not eat anything today. Now she's feeling________.

(a) sleepy

(b) tired

(c) hungry

(d) sad

Space for Rough Work

MATHEMATICS MOCK TEST 1–5

OLYMPIAD
Mock Test 1

Name : _______________

Number of Questions : 40

Max. Marks : 40

Time : 2 Hours

There is no negative marking in the test.

1. Identify the shape made of straight lines.

   (a) 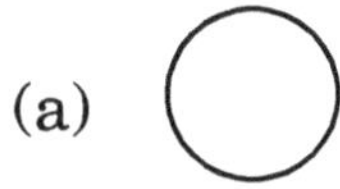

   (b) 

   (c) 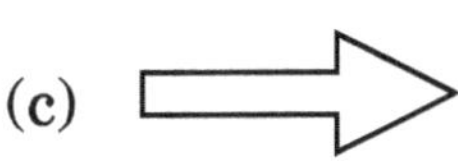

   (d) 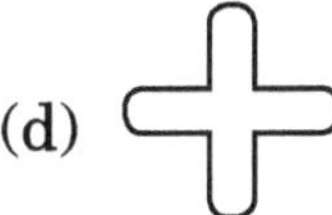

2. Identify the object which rolls.

   (a) 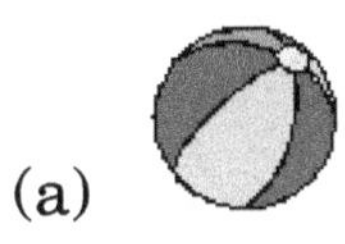

   (b) 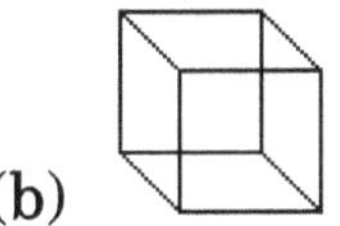

   (c) 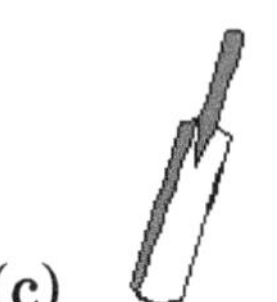

   (d) 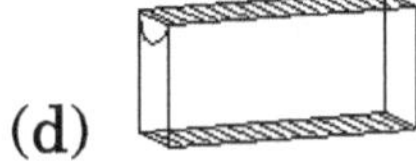

3. Look at the different solid shapes in the given picture, and find the number of objects that has a shape like cuboid.

   (a) 2   (b) 3
   (c) 4   (d) 5

4. The picture spots many monkeys and parrots in the jungle. Choose the correct option given for the number of monkeys in the picture.

Space for Rough Work

(a) 4   (b) 5

(c) 6   (d) 7

5. How many ducks are left if you remove 4 ducks by counting back?

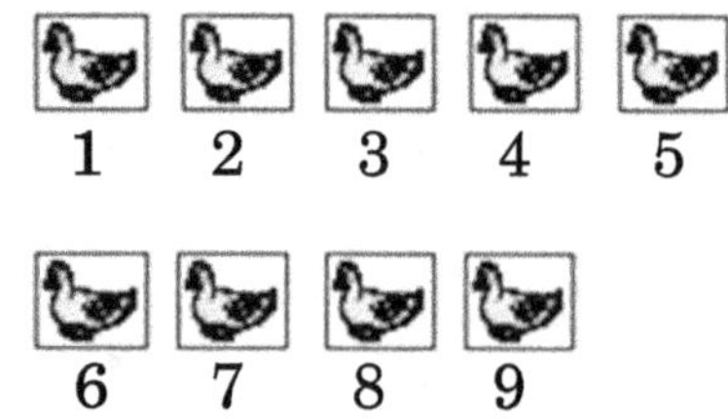

(a) 3   (b) 4

(c) 5   (d) 6

6. There are some objects given in each box and their numbers are given in the brackets associated with the box. Choose the wrong combination of objects and counting.

(a)  (6)

(b) 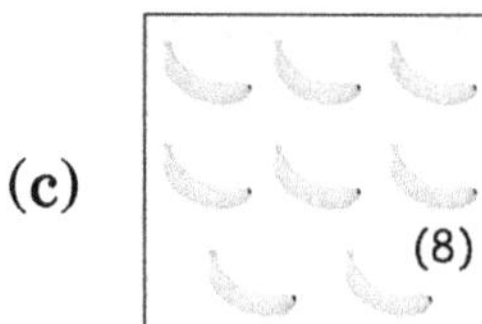 (5)

(c) 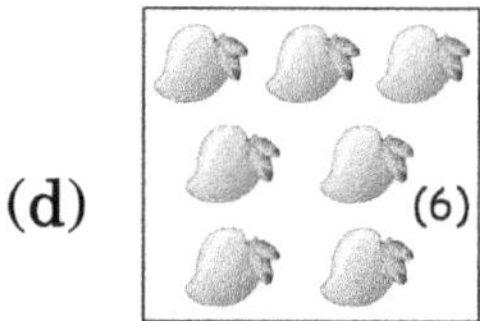 (8)

(d) (6)

7. Add the balls given below and choose the correct option.

(a) 4   (b) 5

(c) 6   (d) 7

8. Which of the following are written in order from smallest to greatest?

(a) | 16 | 32 | 31 | 23 |

(b) | 23 | 31 | 16 | 32 |

(c) | 16 | 23 | 31 | 32 |

(d) | 32 | 31 | 23 | 16 |

9. Tiya draws 2 smileys on the sand near the pond and Tarun draws some more smileys. Now there are 5 smileys in all. Then, smileys drawn by the Tarun are equal to?

(a) 3   (b) 2

(c) 4   (d) 1

10. Gungun has 7 candies. She gets 1 more from her father. How many candies does she have now?

(a) 6   (b) 7

(c) 8   (d) 9

11. Krish had 7 toy cars. He broke 2 of them while playing. How many toy cars are left with him? Use the number line and choose the correct option:

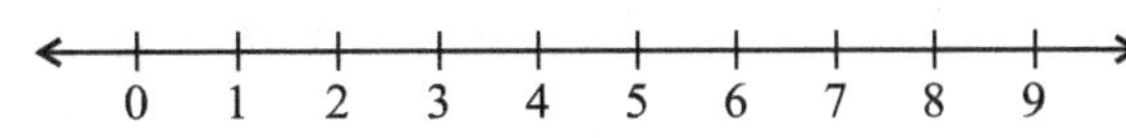

(a) 3   (b) 6

(c) 5   (d) 4

12. 7 people are sitting in a taxi. After one stop, 3 people get down. How many people continued the journey?

(a) 4   (b) 3

(c) 2   (d) 5

13. Match the bats in column-A with balls in column-B.

Column-A	Column-B
A. $9 - 9$	(i) 
B. $8 - 1$	(ii) 
C. $7 - 6$	(iii) 
D. $4 + 2$	(iv)

Space for Rough Work

	A	B	C	D
(a)	(iii)	(iv)	(i)	(ii)
(b)	(iv)	(i)	(iii)	(ii)
(c)	(ii)	(iii)	(i)	(iv)
(d)	(iv)	(iii)	(ii)	(i)

14. A hen lays 7 eggs in a week. A man takes away all the eggs. How many eggs are left there?

    (a) Two   (b) Eight

    (c) Six   (d) Zero

15. Rimjhim has 4 dolls. Her mother gave her 2 teddy bears and her father gave her 1 toy car on her birthday. How many toys does she have?

    (a) 6   (b) 5

    (c) 9   (d) 7

16. A box with some numbers is given below. Find out how many numbers are there in the box less than 10 ?

10	6	9	14	12
1	11	8	2	15

    (a) 4   (b) 6

    (c) 5   (d) 8

17. Choose the correct option to complete the number line.

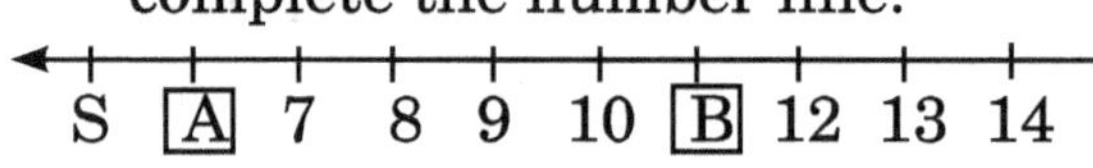

    (a) A = 5, B = 12

    (b) A = 6, B = 11

    (c) A = 4, B = 13

    (d) A = 5, B = 11

18. Ziya is celebrating her birthday today. 6 friends have come to the party. 7 more are yet to come. How many friends will be there?

(a) 13   (b) 17

(c) 14   (d) 15

19. 5 children are sitting in the school bus. 6 more children get into the bus at one stop. After some time, 2 more children get into the bus. How many children are there in the bus now?

(a) 11   (b) 13

(c) 14   (d) 15

20. Jay is at 16 on the number line. Where does he end up on the number line after counting 8 steps backwards?

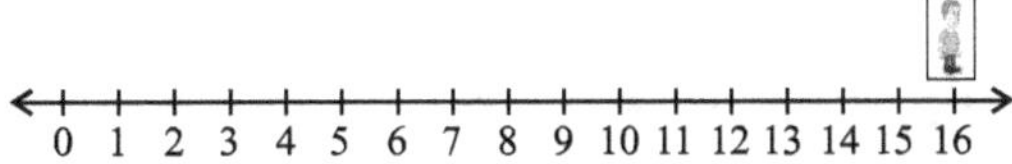

(a) 7   (b) 14

(c) 8   (d) 9

21. Who am I?

I lie between 37 and 43.

I have 0 ones.

What number am I?

(a) 30   (b) 40

(c) 50   (d) 60

22. Honeybee wants to write the smallest number at the centre of the flower. Help her to do so by choosing the correct option.

(a) 64   (b) 45

(c) 73   (d) 59

23. Chintu buys 32 mangoes, 24 bananas, 45 oranges and 40 guavas. Which fruit does Chintu buy the least?

(a) Mango   (b) Banana

(c) Orange   (d) Guava

24. Riya has 14 pencils and her friend Rupal has 19 pencils. How many more pencils does Rupal has?

(a) 4   (b) 6

(c) 5   (d) 7

25. Anjali makes groups of 10 pencils each from the given pencils. How many pencils will be left?

(a) 5   (b) 7

(c) 4   (d) 3

26. Which container holds more water? Choose the correct option.

(a) 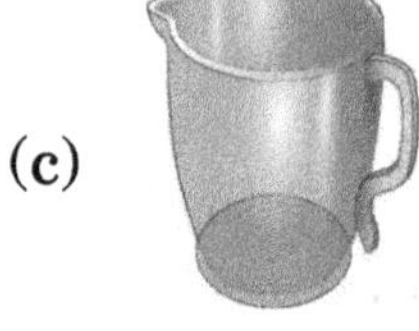   (b) 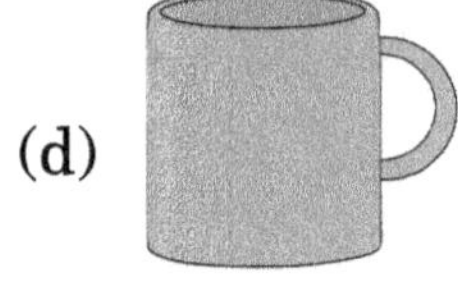

(c)   (d)

27. Add the money and choose the correct option.

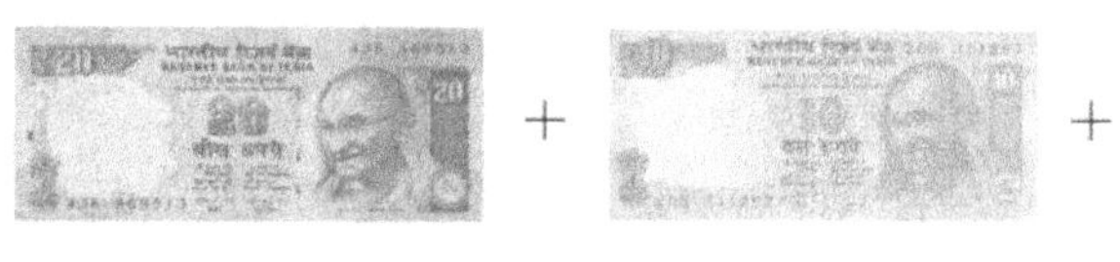

(a) ₹ 80   (b) ₹ 75

(c) ₹ 85   (d) ₹ 65

28. Calculate the value of a fruit basket and choose the correct option.

(a) ₹ 55   (b) ₹ 53

(c) ₹ 47   (d) ₹ 57

29. The length of the pencil is about ☐ paper clips.

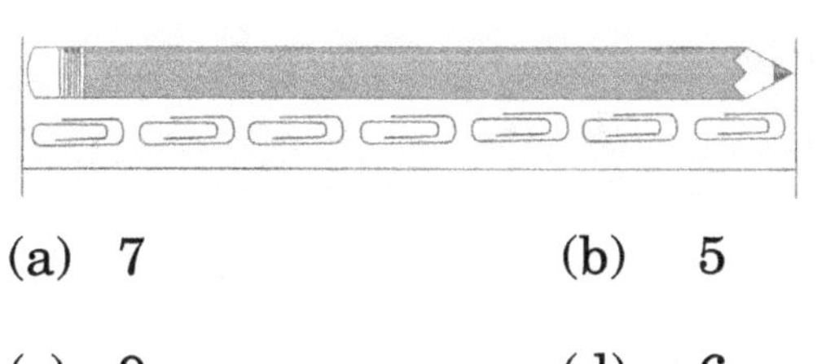

(a) 7   (b) 5

(c) 9   (d) 6

Directions (Qs. 30 to 32): Look at the diagram carefully and answer the questions that follows.

30. How many fishes have stripes in the pond?

(a) 3   (b) 5

(c) 4   (d) 6

31. How many fishes are swimming in left direction?

(a) 8   (b) 9

(c) 7   (d) 10

32. How many fishes are there in total?

(a) 13   (b) 14

(c) 15   (d) 16

33. Complete the pattern by choosing the correct option.

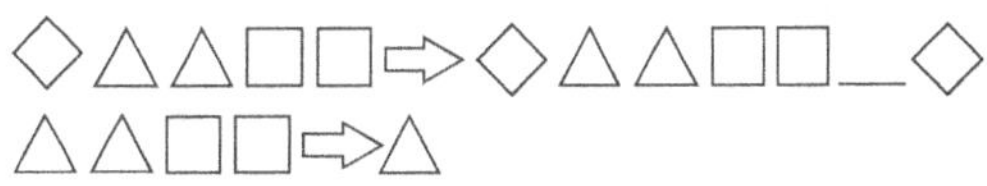

(a) ☐   (b) △

(c) ◇   (d) ⇨

Space for Rough Work

34. Look at the pattern.

○△△○△△○△△○△△○△△○

Now identify the pattern that is similar to the given pattern.

(a) 

(b) ▭▫▫▭▫▫▭▫▫▭▫▫▭▫▫

(c) →○→○→○→○→○→○→○

(d) ☹☺☹☺☹☺☹☺☹☺☹☺☹☺☹☺

35. Ronald was born in the month that comes after the tenth month of the year. In which month was Ronald born?

(a) September (b) October

(c) November (d) December

36. Which number is shown on the abacus?

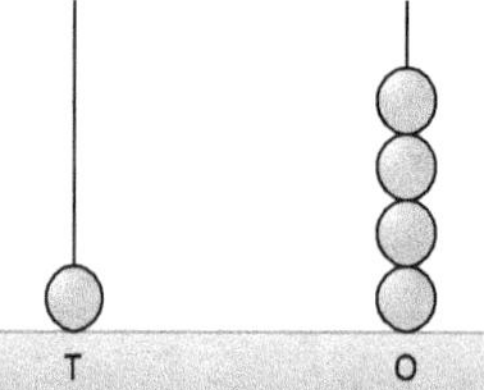

(a) 13 (b) 14

(c) 41 (d) 31

37. Look at the picture. Compare the weight of different objects and choose the option which is lightest.

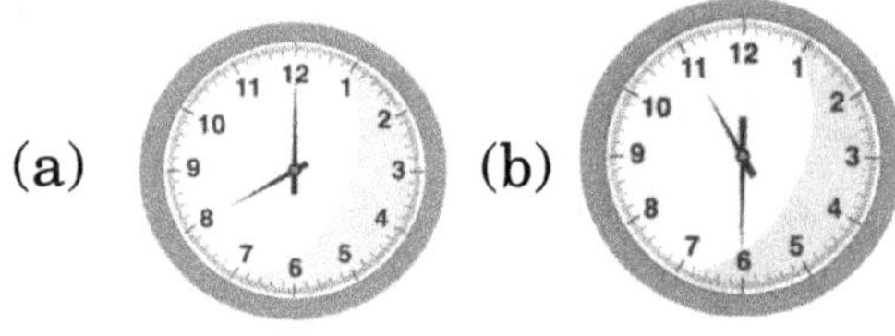

(a) Apple (b) Pumpkin

(c) Strawberry (d) Watermelon

38. Choose the clock that is showing 7 o'clock.

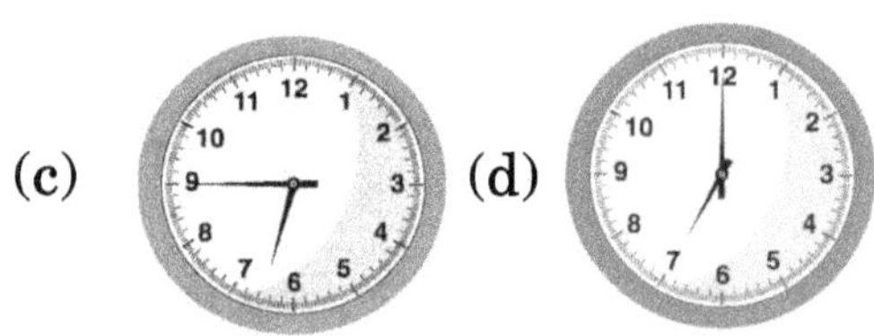

(a) (b)

(c) (d)

Space for Rough Work
---

39. Which of the following is not a solid?

(a) 

(b)

(c)

(d)

40. Look at the picture, add the numbers and choose the number name you will get from the given options.

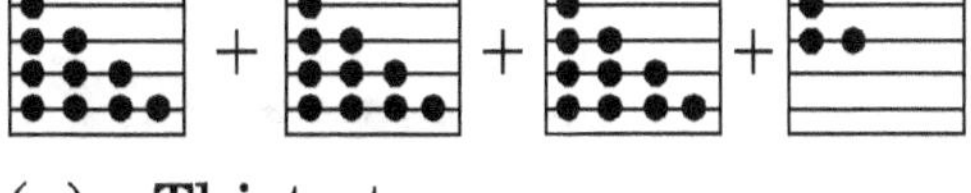

(a) Thirty-two

(b) Forty-three

(c) Twenty-three

(d) Thirty-three

Name : _________

Max. Marks : 40

Number of Questions : 40

Time : 2 Hours

There is no negative marking in the test.

1. What comes in between 2 and 4?

  (a) 7   (b) 5

  (c) 6   (d) 3

2. Choose the correct option.

  (a) $4 + 2 = 6$ (b) $3 + 4 = 7$

  (c) $5 + 3 = 8$ (d) $6 + 2 = 8$

3. There are eight birds sitting on the branch of a tree. Four flew away. How many birds are left on the branch of the tree?

  (a) 4   (b) 5

  (c) 7   (d) 6

4. How many circles are there in the given picture?

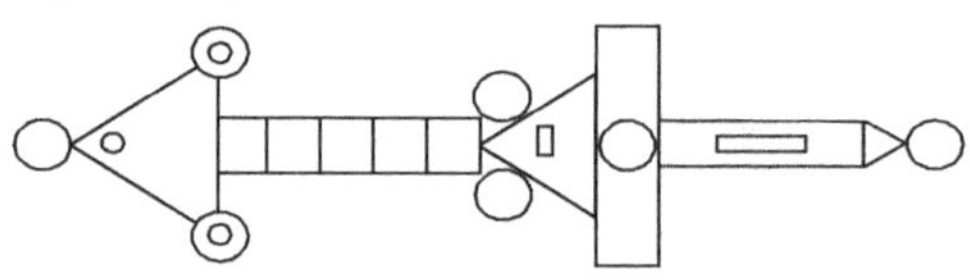

  (a) 9   (b) 10

  (c) 12   (d) 8

———————————— Space for Rough Work ————————————

5. Look at the diagram and fill in the blank by choosing the correct option.

The mat is ☐ paces long.

(a) 5   (b) 6

(c) 4   (d) 8

6. Choose the vessel that can contain more glasses of water.

(a) 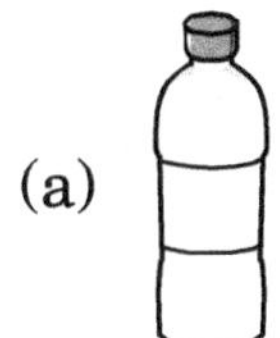   (b) 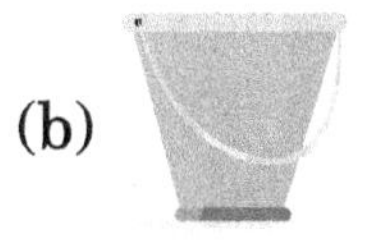

(c) 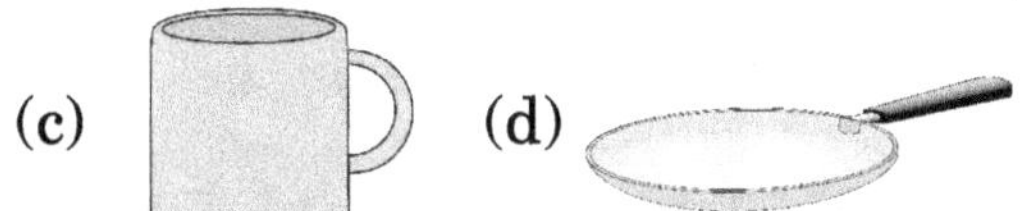   (d)

7. Choose the correct option.

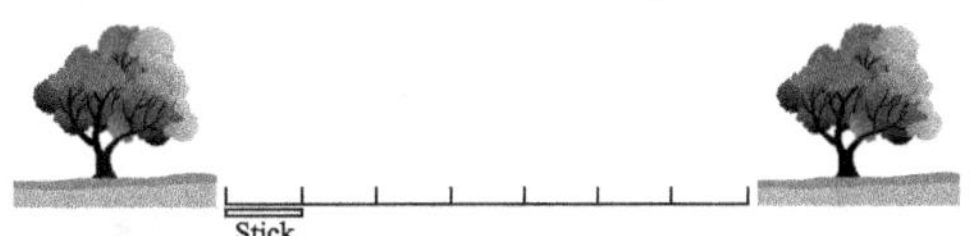

The distance between the two trees is ☐ sticks.

(a) 5   (b) 6

(c) 7   (d) 8

8. Sachin collected money from his neighbours for donation. What amount did he collect ?

(a) ₹ 36   (b) ₹ 38

(c) ₹28   (d) ₹ 48

9. Sunny buys four chocolates. Each chocolate costs ₹ 5.

He pays a total of ₹ _____.

(a) 15   (b) 25
(c) 20   (d) 30

10. Read and tell the time.

(a) 6 : 00   (b) 6 : 05
(c) 2 : 30   (d) 9 : 00

11. Look at the pattern.

Now identify the pattern that is similar to the given pattern.

(a) →☐☐ →☐☐ →☐☐ →☐☐ -

(b) ✸✸✸☆☆✸✸✸☆☆

(c) ƁƷƁƷƁƷ ƁƷ ƁƷ

(d) ABC ABC ABC ABC

12. Look at the picture. Compare the weight of different objects and choose the option which is heaviest.

(a) 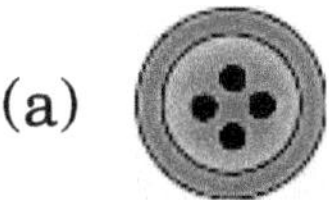   (b) 

(c) 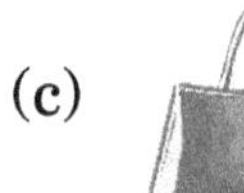   (d) 

13. The day that comes before Friday but after Wednesday is

(a) Tuesday   (b) Thursday
(c) Saturday   (d) Sunday

14. Tanishk goes to school at 08 : 00 in the morning. Help him to find the correct time in the watch by choosing the correct option.

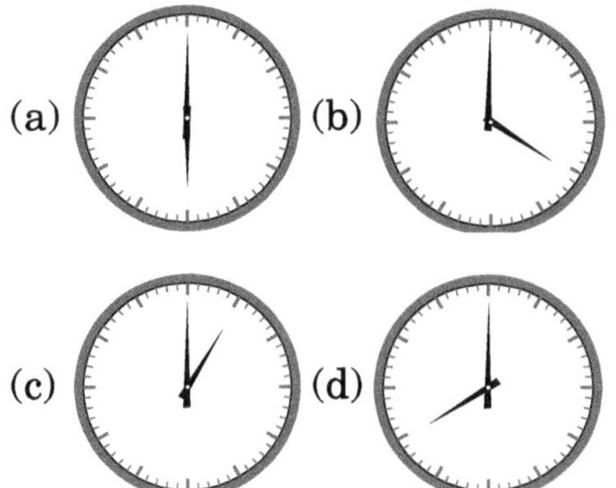

15. Follow the arrows and fill the box.

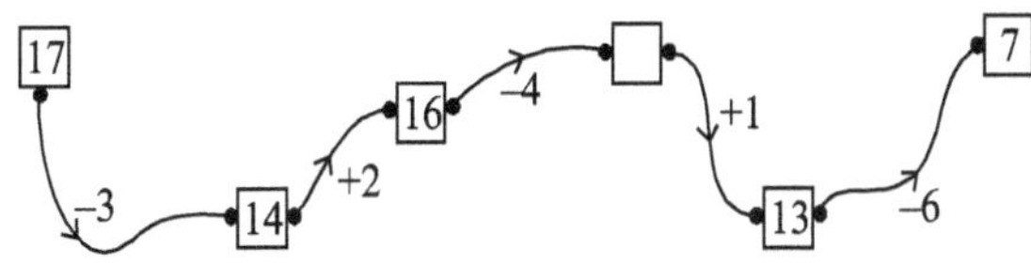

(a) 18   (b) 15

(c) 12   (d) 20

16. Rita buys 78 ice creams. Out of them 25 melted. How many are left ?

(a) 63   (b) 53

(c) 43   (d) 50

17. A fruit seller sold 38 apples on Monday and 41 apples on Tuesday. How many did he sell altogether in two days ?

(a) 79   (b) 69

(c) 3   (d) 99

18. Which of the following is a solid shape?

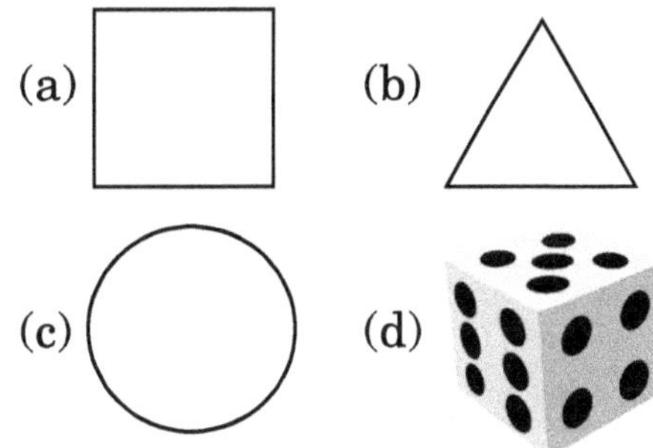

(a) ▢   (b) △

(c) ◯   (d) [dice]

19. Which of the following are in order from greatest to smallest?

(a)

34	47	50	11

(b)

11	37	47	50

(c)

50	11	47	34

(d)

50	47	34	11

Space for Rough Work

20. Aisha has 3 leaves. She needs 8 leaves to paste in her scrapbook. Akram gives her some more leaves so that he has eight leaves. How many leaves does Akram give her?

    (a) 4   (b) 5

    (c) 6   (d) 7

21. Use the number line to subtract and fill in the blanks.

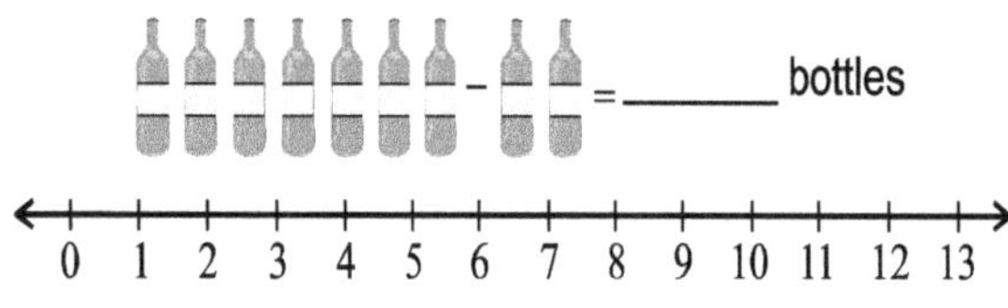

(a) 4   (b) 5

(c) 6   (d) 3

22. Aditi had 6 marbles. She lost some marbles. Now she has only 4. How many marbles did she loose ?

    (a) 3   (b) 1

    (c) 2   (d) 4

23. Tiya is 7 years old. Her brother is 5 years elder to her. How old is he?

    (a) 10 years   (b) 11 years

    (c) 12 years   (d) 14 years

24. There are some butterflies in a garden. 3 flew away as I ran towards them. Now I can see only 6. How many butterflies were there in the beginning?

    (a) 9   (b) 10

    (c) 8   (d) 11

25. I am a two digit number between 75 and 80. I have 7 tens and 6 ones. What number am I ?

    (a) 67   (b) 78

    (c) 79   (d) 76

26. Find the number represented on the abacus and choose the correct option.

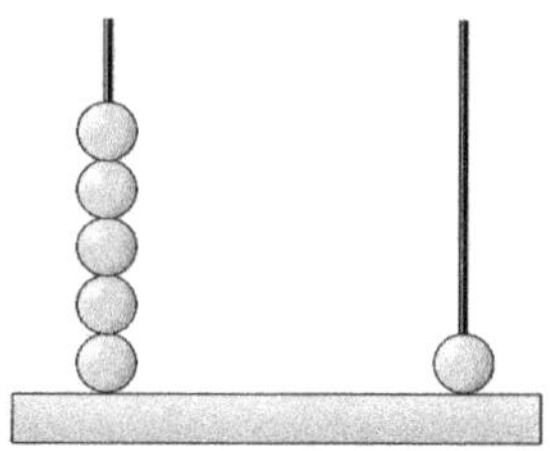

(a) Forty-two   (b) Fifty-two

(c) Fifty-nine   (d) Fifty-one

Space for Rough Work

27. Look at the picture.

Basket-1   Basket-2   Basket-3

How many mangoes are there in all ?

(a) 18   (b) 19

(c) 20   (d) 22

28. Choose the correct abacus representing number 36.

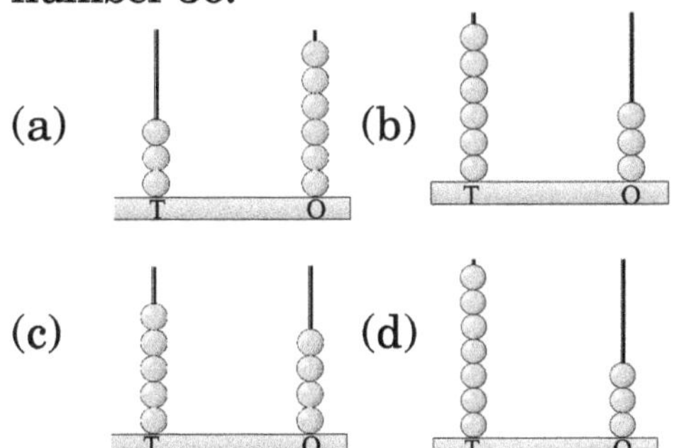

(a)   (b)

(c)   (d)

29. Look at the shapes and choose the object that rolls.

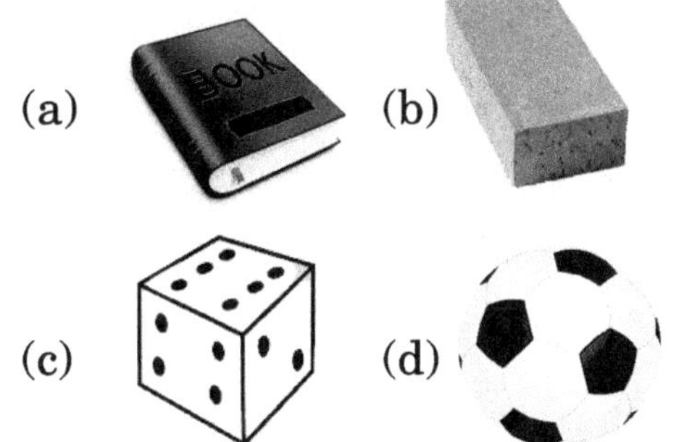

(a)   (b)

(c)   (d)

30. Saurabh and his friends collected money for their school charity-fund.

Total amount collected by them is

(a) ₹ 98   (b) ₹ 88

(c) ₹ 78   (d) ₹ 80

Directions (Qs. 31 to 33): Look at the given picture and answer the following questions.

31. How many mangoes are there in the basket ?

(a) 3   (b) 4

(c) 5   (d) 6

Space for Rough Work

32. Which fruit is maximum in number ?

    (a) Apple   (b) Mango

    (c) Banana   (d) Watermelon

33. How many fruits are there in total?

    (a) 16   (b) 17

    (c) 18   (d) 19

34. Choose the wrong option.

    (a) January is the first month of the year.

    (b) May is the fifth month of the year.

    (c) December is the last month of the year.

    (d) The month between September and November is August.

35. Rahul has 35 shirts. His brother has 12 shirts. How many shirts do they have together ?

    (a) 18   (b) 23

    (c) 47   (d) 65

36. Which of the following is heaviest?

    (a)    (b)

    (c) 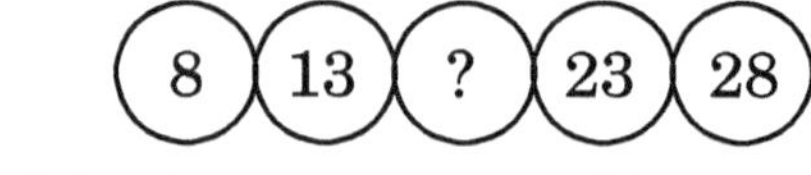   (d)

37. A bus is carrying 54 passengers. 23 of them get off at a bus stand. The number of passenger left is

    (a) 17   (b) 37

    (c) 31   (d) 25

38. What comes in the blank circle ?

    8 13 ? 23 28

    (a) 9   (b) 18

    (c) 10   (d) 15

39. Complete the subtraction. Choose the correct number to find the answer.

    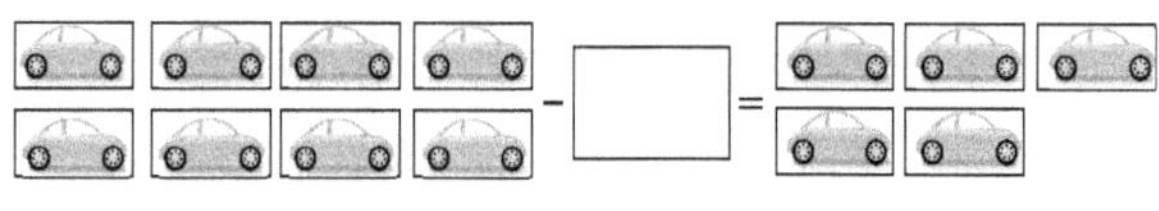

    (a) 2   (b) 5

    (c) 3   (d) 4

40. 10 children are playing in the park. 5 more children join them. How many children are playing in the park now ?

Tens	Ones
1	0
+	5

(a) 6

(b) 15

(c) 5

(d) 20

OLYMPIAD
Mock Test

Name : __________

Number of Questions : 35

Max. Marks : 35

Time : 2 Hours

There is no negative marking in the test.

1. Find the number that comes in between

   (a) 18   (b) 22

   (c) 20   (d) 30

2. Look at the pictures.

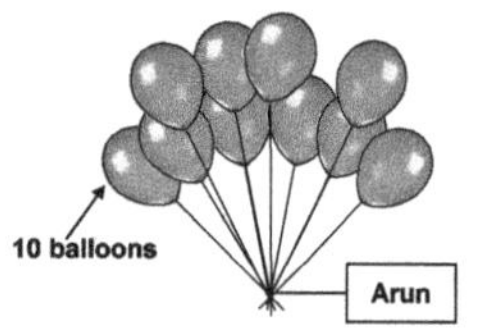

   Arun has ______ balloons more than Varun.

   (a) 2   (b) 3

   (c) 4   (d) 1

3. Choose the wrong option.

   (a) December is the last month of the year.

   (b) June is the second month of the year.

   (c) May comes between April and June.

   (d) July comes before August.

4. The height of tree =

   (a) 7 units   (b) 6 units

   (c) 8 units   (d) 5 units

Space for Rough Work

5.   Choose the correct option:

(a) $3 + 2 = 5$ (b) $4 + 6 = 10$

(c) $6 + 3 = 9$ (d) $4 + 4 = 8$

6.   There are 4 apples in the basket.

3 oranges are added to the same basket.

There are _______ fruits in the basket.

(a) 7   (b) 8

(c) 6   (d) 5

7.   Put the correct number in the circle.

(a) 4   (b) 3

(c) 5   (d) 6

8.   19 bees were in a beehive. 12 bees flew away.

How many bees were left in the beehive ?

(a) 31   (b) 8

(c) 7   (d) 5

9.   Neelam has 10 roses.

She gives 3 to her friend.

How many roses are left with her?

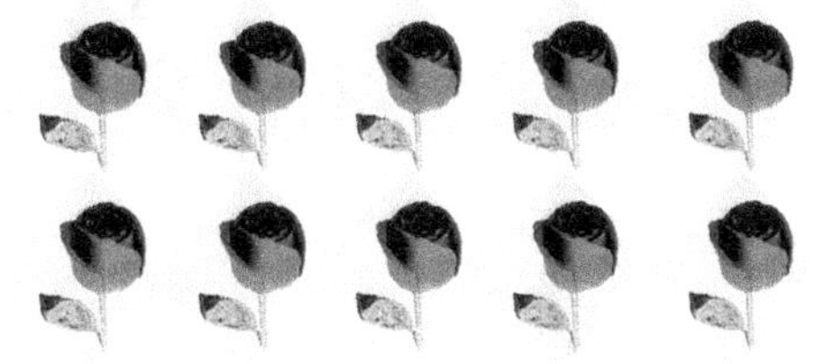

(a) 6   (b) 7

(c) 8   (d) 9

_______________________ *Space for Rough Work* _______________________

10. Choose the object which has a rectangular shape.

(a) 

(b) 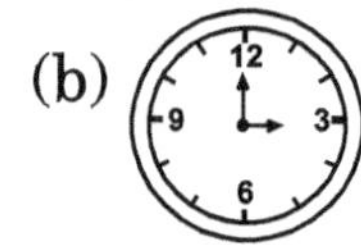

(c) 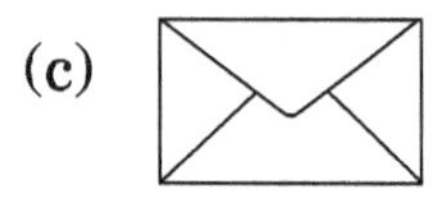

(d) 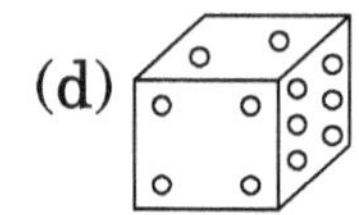

11. See the pattern and choose the correct missing image.

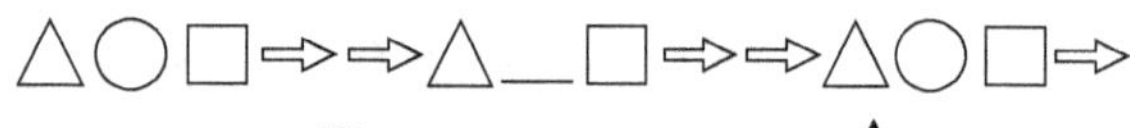

(a) ◯

(b) △

(c) ☐

(d) ⇨

12. Match the geometrical shape to which the object most closely resembles.

(A) 

(i) 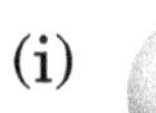

(B) 

(ii) 

(C) 

(iii) 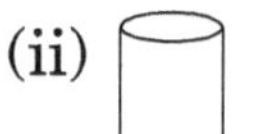

(D) 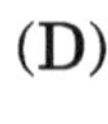
Book

(iv) 

(a) A-(iv); B-(ii); C-(iii); D-(i)

(b) A-(iii); B-(i); C-(ii); D-(iv)

(c) A-(i); B-(iv); C-(iii); D-(ii)

(d) A-(iv); B-(i); C-(ii); D-(iii)

13. Count and choose the correct option.

1 bunch of 10 lilies each and 7 loose lilies.

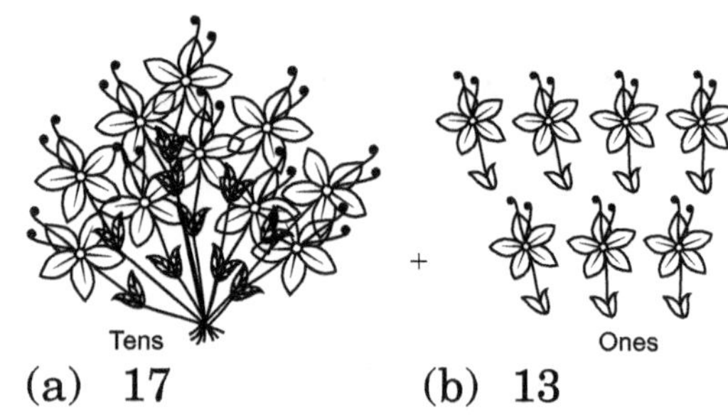

(a) 17

(b) 13

(c) 27

(d) 8

14. Choose the correct option, which shows the numbers in decreasing order.

(a) 12 32 24 65 86

(b) 86 65 32 24 12

(c) 12 24 32 65 86

(d) 86 32 65 12 24

—————————— Space for Rough Work ——————————

15. Choose the wrong statement.

    (a) Thursday comes after Wednesday.

    (b) Saturday comes between Friday and Sunday.

    (c) Tuesday is the second day of the week.

    (d) Sunday is the first day of week.

16. Santa Claus comes to town riding on his sleigh. Which month is this?

    (a) October   (b) November

    (c) December   (d) January

17. Arjun opened his money box and found these notes and coins. How much money did he has ?

    (a) ₹ 48   (b) ₹ 58

    (c) ₹ 56   (d) ₹ 64

18. Choose the amount that is available in both note and coin.

    (a) ₹ 100   (b) ₹ 50

    (c) ₹ 10   (d) ₹ 20

19. Choose the bag that has more money.

(a)

(b)

(c)

(d)

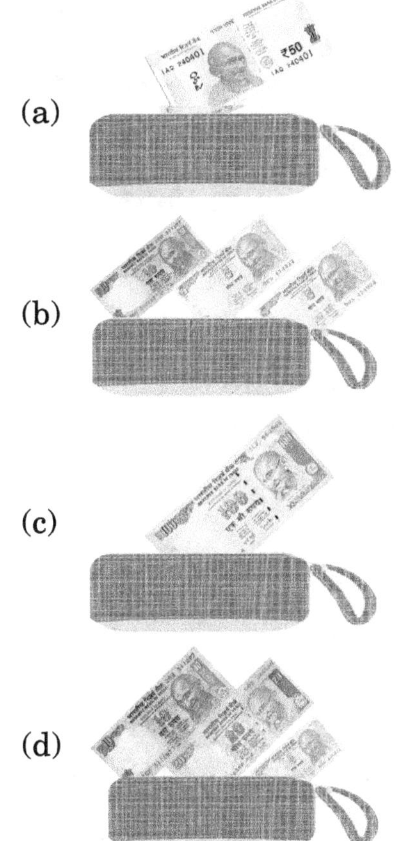

―――――――― *Space for Rough Work* ――――――――

20. $7 + 7 + 7 + 7 + 7 + 7 = \boxed{} \times 7$

(a) 7   (b) 6

(c) 5   (d) 4

21. There are 24 girls are 28 boys in a class. How many students are there in all?

(a) 42   (b) 52

(c) 14   (d) 32

22. Choose the correct number - name for the number shown on the abacus.

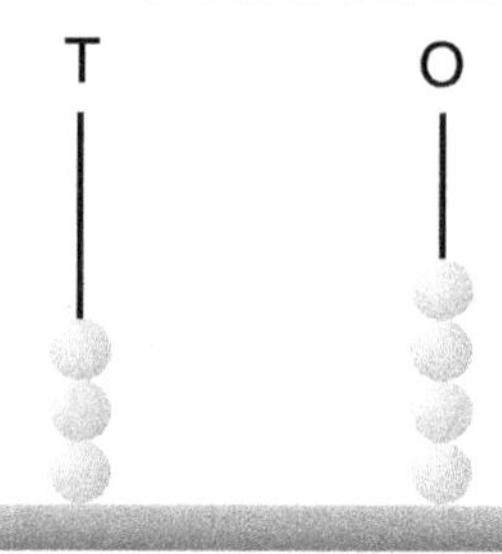

(a) Forty four   (b) Thirty four

(c) Thirty three   (d) Forty three

23. Varun makes some shapes using straight and curved lines. Choose the shape which is not made up of curved lines.

(a) 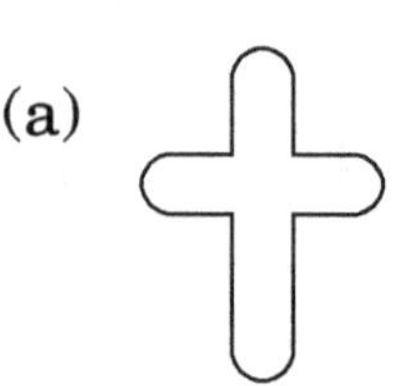   (b) 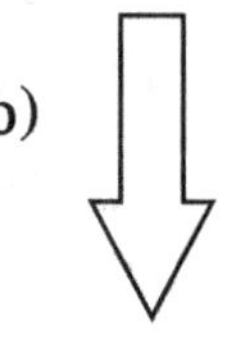

(c)    (d) 

24. 24 parrots are sitting on a tree. 4 more parrots come and sit on the tree. How many parrots are now sitting on the tree ?

(a) 28   (b) 27

(c) 20   (d) 12

25. Choose the correct option to complete the subtraction.

$7 - 0 = \underline{}$

(a) 1   (b) 7

(c) 0   (d) 4

Space for Rough Work

26. Find the number.

I am an odd number.

When you add my 2 digits, the total is 6.

I am less than 20.

(a) 12   (b) 16

(c) 51   (d) 15

27. There are 3 bunches of ten grapes each and 5 loose grapes. How many grapes are there in total ?

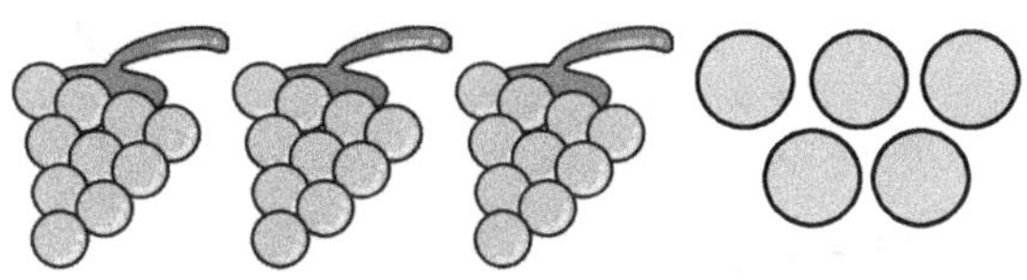

(a) 35   (b) 33

(c) 45   (d) 25

28. There are 40 big and 26 small fishes in a pond.
How many fishes are there in all ?

(a) 46   (b) 56

(c) 66   (d) 76

29. Which of the following is lightest?

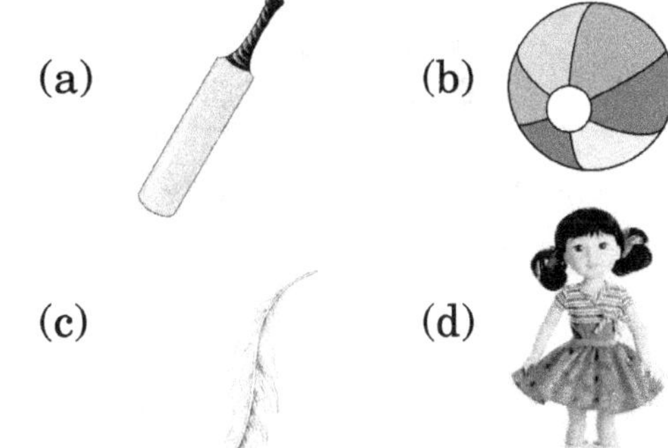

(a)   (b)

(c)   (d)

30. Choose the time shown by clock.

(a) 12 o'clock   (b) 6 o'clock

(c) 4 o'clock   (d) 9 o'clock

Directions (Q. 31 to 33): Look at the picture and answer the questions given below.

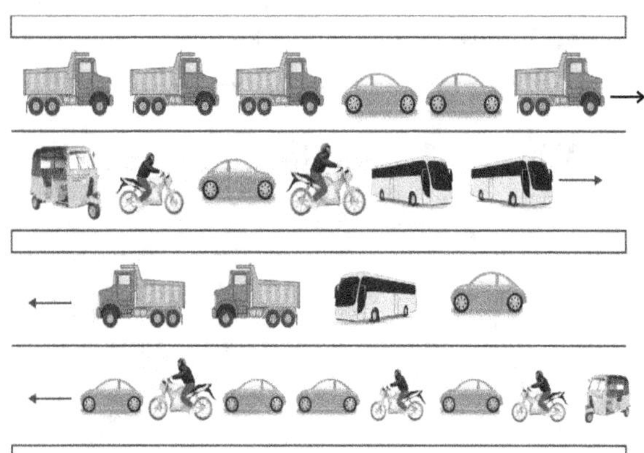

31. How many cars are there on the road ?

    (a) 11   (b) 10

    (c) 8   (d) 9

32. What kind of vehicles are the least?

    (a) Car   (b) Bike

    (c) Truck   (d) Auto

33. How many more trucks than buses are on the road ?

    (a) 2   (b) 3

    (c) 4   (d) 5

34. Arrange these numbers starting from the smallest on the lowest step to the biggest on the top of the steps. Then choose the correct option from smaller to bigger.

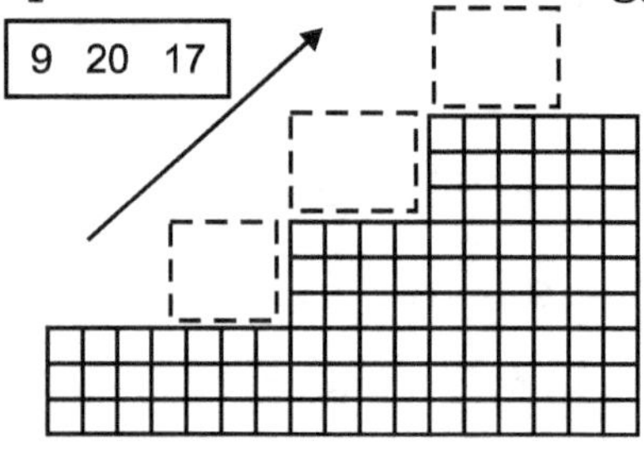

    (a) 9, 20, 17   (b) 9, 17, 20

    (c) 17, 20, 9   (d) 20, 9, 17

35. The number name for 96 is

    (a) Eighty-Six   (b) Sixty-Nine

    (c) Sixty-Six   (d) Ninety-Six

Space for Rough Work

OLYMPIAD
Mock Test 4

Name : ___________

Number of Questions : 35

Max. Marks : 35

Time : 2 Hours

There is no negative marking in the test.

1. Seventy nine can be written as _______ .

   (a) 7 + 9   (b) 7 + 90

   (c) 70 + 90   (d) 70 + 9

2. 4 tens and 2 ones is _______ .

   (a) 40   (b) 24

   (c) 42   (d) 48

3. Which of the following holds more milk?

   (a)    (b)

   (c)    (d) 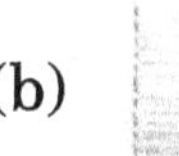

4. 44 is _______ 4 + 4.

   (a) greater than

   (b) less than

   (c) equal to

   (d) none of these

5. A balloon seller has 13 green, 2 orange and 3 red balloons. Find the total number of balloons.

   (a) 19   (b) 16

   (c) 18   (d) 20

6. Find the total number of fruits?

   (a) 10   (b) 11

   (c) 12   (d) 14

Space for Rough Work

7. Nikita counted 12 frogs in a pond. 5 frogs jumped out of the pond. How many frogs are left?

(a) 7 (b) 18

(c) 17 (d) 20

8. There are 10 zebras, 13 elephants and 15 tigers in a zoo. How many total number of animals are there in the zoo?

(a) 38 (b) 48

(c) 58 (d) 41

9. There are 18 chocolates in a tray, out of which 3 are eaten by Ravi. How many chocolates are left?

(a) 15 (b) 13

(c) 18 (d) 10

10. There are 45 students in class 4. 8 students were absent on Wednesday. How many students were present on Wednesday?

(a) 42 (b) 62

(c) 82 (d) 37

11. The length of the scale is about ☐ boxes long.

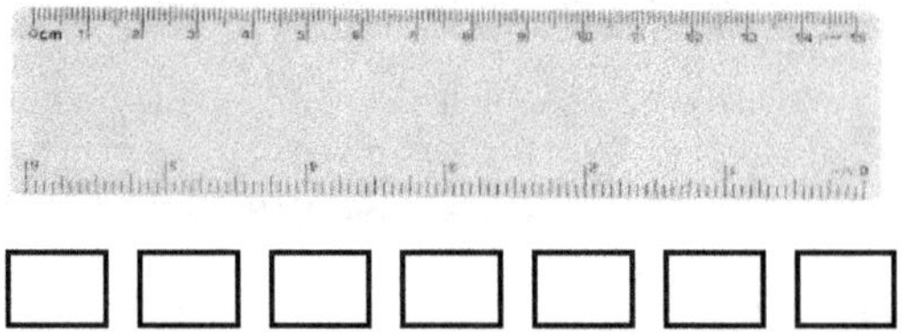

(a) 5 (b) 6

(c) 7 (d) 8

12. 5 pencils + 2 pencil – 1 pencil = ?

(a) 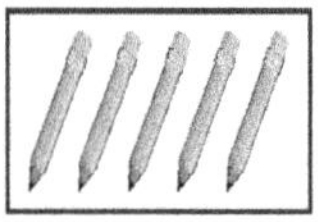

(b) 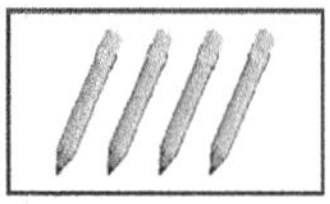

(c) 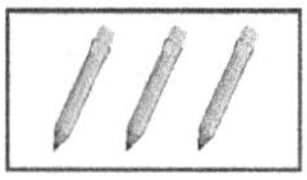

(d) 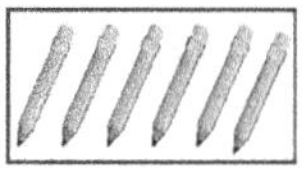

13. Choose the amount that is available in both note and coin.

(a) ₹ 5 (b) ₹ 20

(c) ₹ 50 (d) ₹ 100

Space for Rough Work

14. What is the time shown in the clock?

(a) 12 : 40   (b) 8 : 00

(c) 6 : 00   (d) 7 : 00

15. How many days are there in between Monday and Thursday?

(a) 5   (b) 4

(c) 3   (d) 2

16. Today is Wednesday and yesterday it was Meera's birthday. On which day was her birthday?

(a) Thursday   (b) Monday

(c) Tuesday   (d) Friday

17. Match column (I) with column (II).

	Column (I)		Column (II)
A.		1.	Cone
B.		2.	Cuboid
C.		3.	Sphere
D.		4.	Cube

	A	B	C	D
(a)	3	2	1	4
(b)	2	1	4	3
(c)	3	1	2	4
(d)	1	2	3	4

Space for Rough Work

18. Which of the following objects slides only?

(a)   (b)

(c)   (d)

19. Which of the following is shown on the number line?

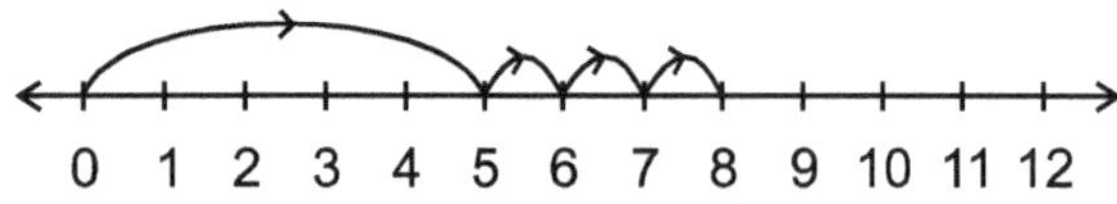

(a) 8 + 5   (b) 5 + 3

(c) 4 + 1   (d) 7 + 1

20.

The fruit basket is kept ________ the table.

(a) below   (b) under

(c) in   (d) on

21. Shreya has 69 fruit cakes. She gave 25 fruit cakes to her friends. How many fruit cakes are left with her?

(a) 33   (b) 44

(c) 54   (d) 36

22. The cost of a pencil box is ₹ 15. What is the cost of 2 pencil boxes?

(a) ₹ 10   (b) ₹ 16

(c) ₹ 30   (d) ₹ 14

23. Which of the following is a flat shape?

(a)    (b) 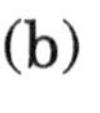

(c) 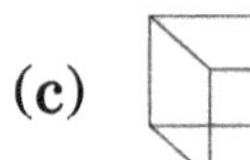   (d) 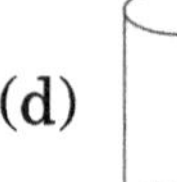

Space for Rough Work

24. Count the money.

(a) ₹ 63   (b) ₹ 72

(c) ₹ 75   (d) ₹ 60

S. No.	Name of the students	Star
1.	Simran	☆ ☆
2.	Shelly	☆ ☆ ☆
3.	Abhishek	☆ ☆ ☆ ☆ ☆
4.	Nitin	☆
5.	Shreya	☆ ☆ ☆ ☆

25. Which of the following month comes just after the fifth month of the year?

(a) May   (b) August

(c) April   (d) June

Directions (Qs 26 to 29): The picture graph shows the number of stars each student has got in class 2. Read and answer the following questions.

26. Who has got the least number of stars?

(a) Simran   (b) Nitin

(c) Shreya   (d) Shelly

27. How many stars did Abhishek get?

(a) 5   (b) 4

(c) 3   (d) 2

28. Who got 4 stars?

(a) Shreya   (b) Nitin

(c) Simran   (d) Abhishek

———————— Space for Rough Work ————————

29. How many students got stars?

    (a) 4   (b) 5

    (c) 6   (d) 3

30. Sheenu brought 24 eggs from a shop. When she returned home she noticed that 4 eggs were broken. How many eggs were in good condition?

    (a) 21   (b) 22

    (c) 20   (d) 24

31. Which of the following is a solid shape?

    (a)    (b) 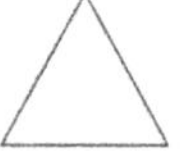

    (c) 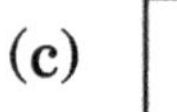   (d) 

32. Rajat has ₹ 50 when he went to a toy store. He selected a motor bike worth ₹ 75. How much amount of money does he require more to buy the motor bike?

    (a) ₹ 50   (b) ₹ 60

    (c) ₹ 70   (d) ₹ 25

33. What comes next in the pattern?

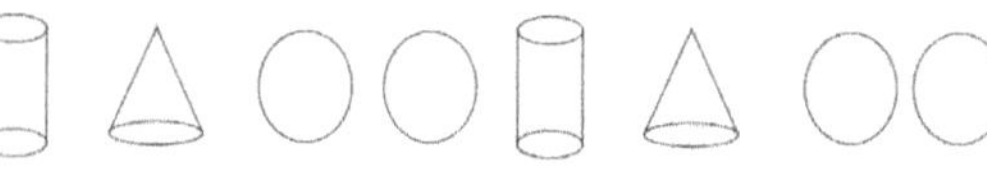

    (a) 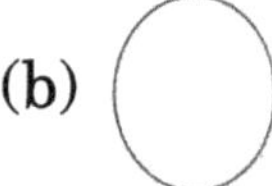   (b)

    (c)   (d)

34. Which of the following shows numbers in order from smallest to greatest?

    (a) 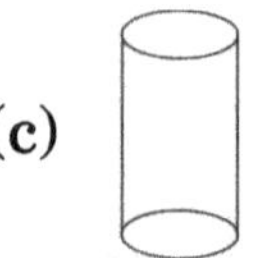

    (b)

    (c)

    (d) 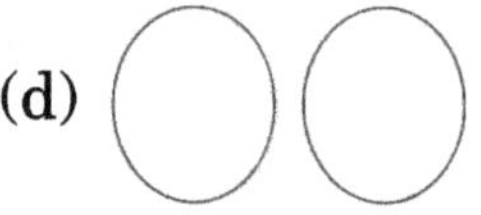

35. Which of the following numbers will give the result?

    24 + ☐ = 29

    (a) 5   (b) 4

    (c) 3   (d) 6

—————————— Space for Rough Work ——————————

OLYMPIAD
Mock Test 5 

Name : __________

Number of Questions : 35

Max. Marks : 35

Time : 2 Hours

There is no negative marking in the test.

1. Which number comes after 6 ?

| 2 | 4 | 6 | | 10 | 12 |

   (a) 8   (b) 7

   (c) 9   (d) 18

2. What comes between 23 and 25?

   21, 22, 23, ________ 25, 26.

   (a) 25   (b) 24

   (c) 27   (d) 28

3. Which of the following months comes before October?

   (a) September   (b) June

   (c) March   (d) April

4. What is the time shown in clock?

   (a) 5 : 00

   (b) 12 : 00

   (c) 4 : 00

   (d) 6 : 00

5. Match List I with List II.

Items (List I)	Shapes (List II)
A.	1. Cuboid
B.	2. Cylinder
C.	3. Sphere
D.	4. Cone

	A	B	C	D
(a)	2	3	1	4
(b)	4	3	2	1
(c)	4	3	1	2
(d)	3	4	1	2

Space for Rough Work

6. See the picture given below and answer the following question.

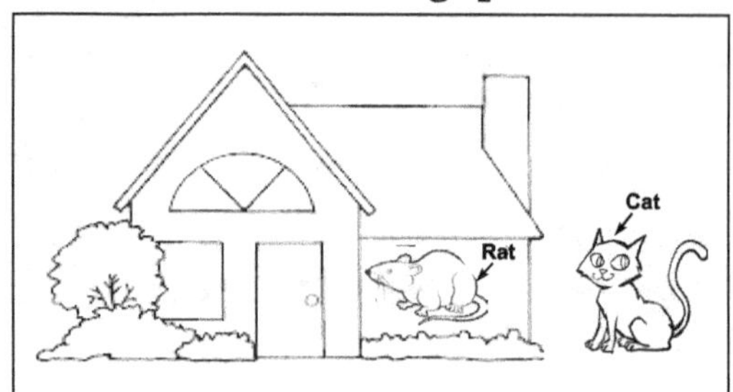

Rat is _______ the house and cat is _______ the house.

(a) after, before

(b) inside, outside

(c) far, near

(d) below, above

7. Find the total number of apples.

(a) 6   (b) 8

(c) 9   (d) 7

8. Which of the following numbers will make the statement correct ?

$$12 + \boxed{} = 20$$

(a) 6   (b) 8

(c) 32   (d) 10

9. Which of the following can't be drawn with the help of a bangle?

(a) Sun   (b) Chapatti

(c) Book   (d) Ring

Directions (Qs. 10 and 11): Read the following sentence and answer the questions given below.

Meera has 15 toffees and 2 apples.

10. How many total number of apples and toffees she have ?

(a) 17   (b) 18

(c) 15   (d) 13

11. She gave 4 toffees to her friend. How many toffees she has now ?

(a) 19   (b) 11

(c) 17   (d) 12

12. Sami has 24 shirts. His father has 15 shirts. How many shirts do they have together?

(a) 39   (b) 40

(c) 38   (d) 41

———— Space for Rough Work ————

Directions (Qs. 13 and 14): Read the following sentence and answer the questions given below.

In a field, there are 5 hens and 3 cows.

13. How many total number of legs of cows are there ?

    (a) 12
    (b) 14
    (c) 16
    (d) 18

14. The total numbers of heads (cows and hens) are

    (a) 8
    (b) 7
    (c) 10
    (d) 5

15. Tina has 64 flowers to make garlands. She uses 35 flowers of them. How many flowers does she have now?

    (a) 39
    (b) 31
    (c) 29
    (d) 41

16. $5 + 5 + 5 + 5 + 5 + 5 + 5 = \boxed{} \times 5$

    (a) 5
    (b) 6
    (c) 7
    (d) 8

17. Which day comes after Wednesday?

    (a) Tuesday
    (b) Thursday
    (c) Sunday
    (d) None of these

Directions (Qs. 18 to 20): Look at the picture and answer the following questions.

18. How many frogs are there in the picture?

    (a) 7
    (b) 6
    (c) 5
    (d) 8

19. How many birds are there in the picture?

    (a) 3
    (b) 4
    (c) 5
    (d) 6

20. How many butterflies are there in the picture?

    (a) 8
    (b) 10
    (c) 9
    (d) 7

Space for Rough Work

21. What comes next in the pattern ?

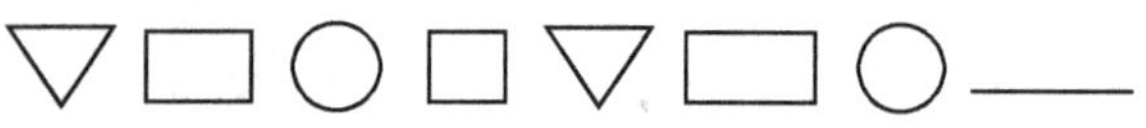

(a)    (b) 

(c)    (d) 

22. Choose the correct option:

(a) Left side is heavier

(b) Right side is heavier

(c) Left side is lighter

(d) None of these

23. Which of the following is longest ?

(a)  Candle

(b) 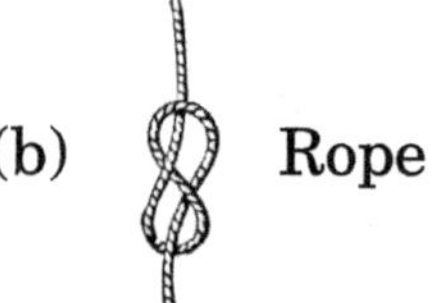 Rope

(c) 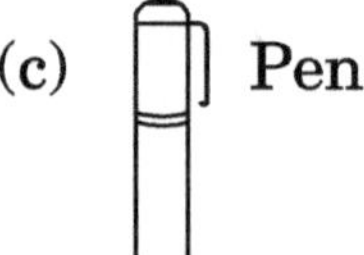 Pen

(d)  Scale

24. Complete the pattern.

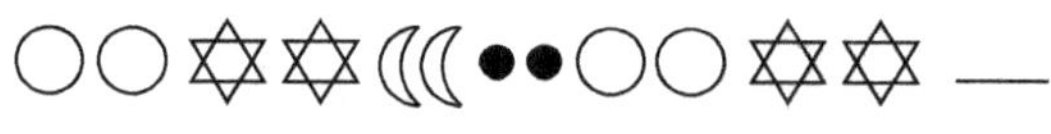

(a) ●   (b) ○

(c) ☾   (d) ✡

25. Calculate the total amount.

is equal to

(a) ₹ 28   (b) ₹ 20

(c) ₹ 31   (d) ₹ 15

Space for Rough Work

26. Which of the following signs will make the statement true?

    20 ☐ **7 = 13**

    (a) –   (b) +

    (c) =   (d) none of these

27. Look at the bowls.

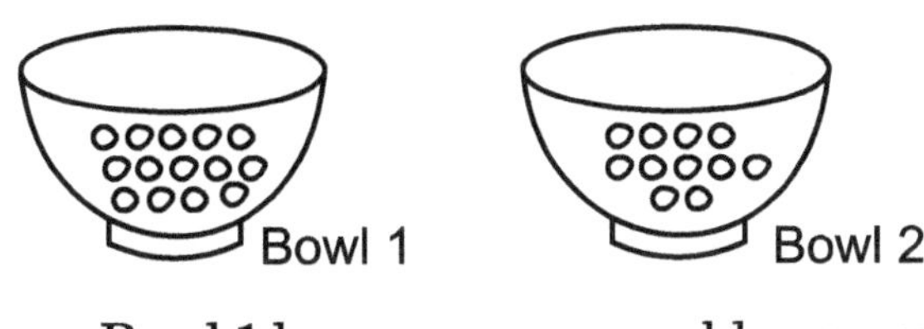

    Bowl 1 has _______ marbles more than Bowl 2.

    (a) 3   (b) 2

    (c) 4   (d) 5

28. Write these numbers in decreasing order.

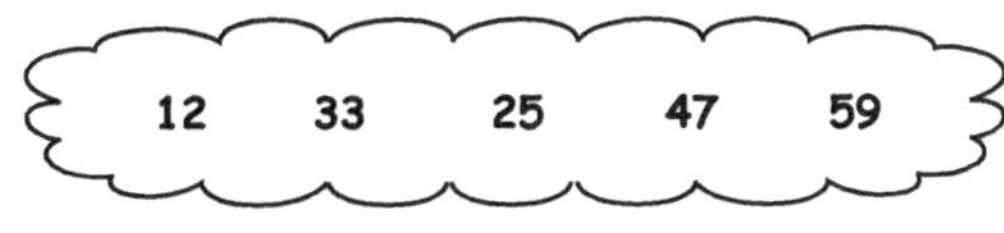

    (a) 59, 33, 25, 47, 12

    (b) 59, 47, 33, 25, 12

    (c) 12, 33, 25, 47, 59

    (d) 33, 47, 25, 12, 59

29. How many straight lines are there in the rectangle ? ☐

    (a) 3   (b) 2

    (c) 4   (d) 5

30. Which of the following letters is made up of curved line ?

    (a) G   (b) E

    (c) F   (d) Y

31. This jug holds _______ cups of water.

    (a) 5   (b) 6

    (c) 4   (d) 7

32. Arrange these numbers in increasing order.

    23 , 77 , 9 , 44 , 93

    (a) 9, 93, 44, 23, 77

    (b) 9, 23, 44, 77, 93

    (c) 9, 44, 93, 23, 77

    (d) 93, 77, 23, 44, 9

Space for Rough Work

Directions (Qs 33 to 35): The data shown in the table shows the birthday of few students of class I. Look at the table and answer the following questions.

	Month	Birthday
(1)	January	5
(2)	February	4
(3)	March	3
(4)	April	2

33. Which of the following months has maximum number of birthdays ?

   (a) January   (b) February

   (c) March   (d) April

34. Which month has minimum number of birthdays?

   (a) January   (b) February

   (c) March   (d) April

35. How many students have their birthdays in the month of March?

   (a) 5   (b) 4

   (c) 2   (d) 3

SCIENCE MOCK TEST 1–5

OLYMPIAD
Mock Test 1

Name : _____________

Number of Questions : 35

Max. Marks : 35

Time : 2 Hours

There is no negative marking in the test.

1. Which one of the following has the characteristic to move from one place to another on its own?

   (a) 

   Plant

   (b) 

   Chair

   (c) 

   House

   (d) 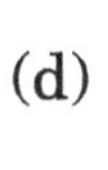

   Tiger

2. Which one of the following is necessary for the growth of a plant?

   (a) Water   (b) Air

   (c) Sunlight   (d) All of these

3. Identify the thing which does not need air, water and food for its growth?

   (a) 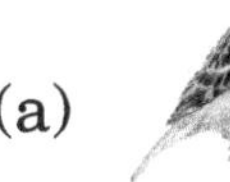

   Sparrow

   (b) 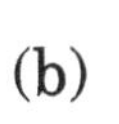

   Squirrel

   (c) 

   Stone

   (d) 

   Rabbit

4. Which of the following clothes we use to wear during the winter season?

   (a) 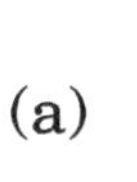

   Shirt

   (b) 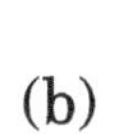

   Sweater

   (c) 

   T-shirt

   (d) 

   Raincoat

———————————— *Space for Rough Work* ————————————

5. Identify the bird from the following.

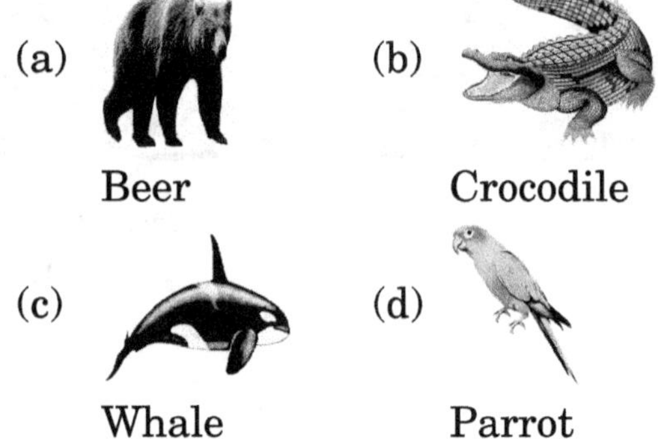

(a) Beer (b) Crocodile (c) Whale (d) Parrot

6. Which one of the following is called the king of fruits?

(a) Mango (b) Apple (c) Papaya (d) Banana

7. Identify the healthy and nutritious food from the following

(a) Burger (b) Pizza (c) Chips (d) Vegetables and fruits

8. Identify the insect from the following.

(a) Lotus (b) Wolf (c) Ant (d) Parrot

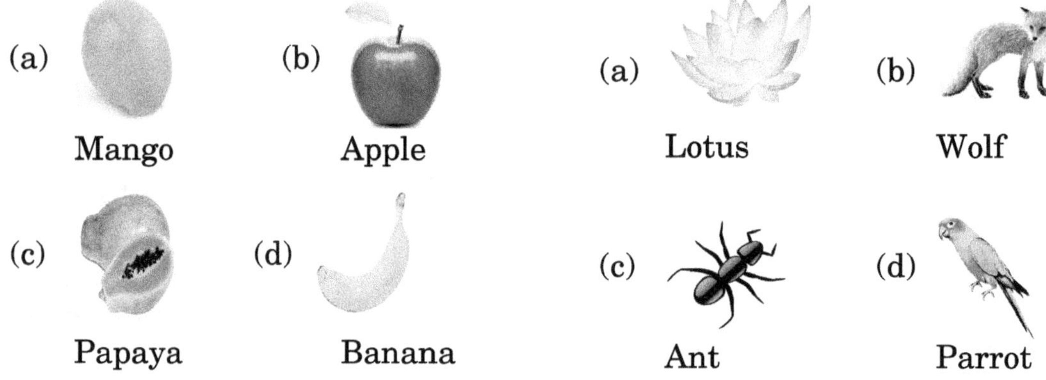

9. What does frog eat?

  (a) Grass   (b) Insect

  (c) Rice   (d) None of these

10. From where day we obtain food grains?

  (a) Plants   (b) Animals

  (c) Humans   (d) All of these

11. Look at the picture and complete the following sentence.

Always cross the road using __________ crossing.

  (a) horse   (b) zebra

  (c) footpath   (d) traffic

12. These are the seeds of____.

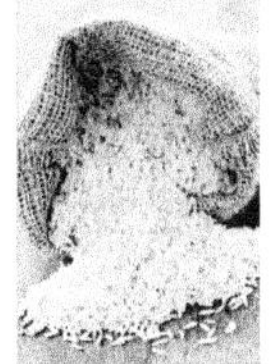

  (a) wheat   (b) rice

  (c) rajma   (d) corn

13. I am green and small. I can make you cry. I am a ________.

  (a) pea   (b) chilli

  (c) ladyfinger   (d) spinach

14. Unscramble the words given below to give the name of the home of the animal shown in the figure.

A T S L B E

  (a) Ebstla   (b) Tebsla

  (c) Stable   (d) Belsta

———————————— Space for Rough Work ————————————

15. Select the correct option.

(a)  lives in water.

(b)  cannot fly.

(c)  has eight legs.

(d) 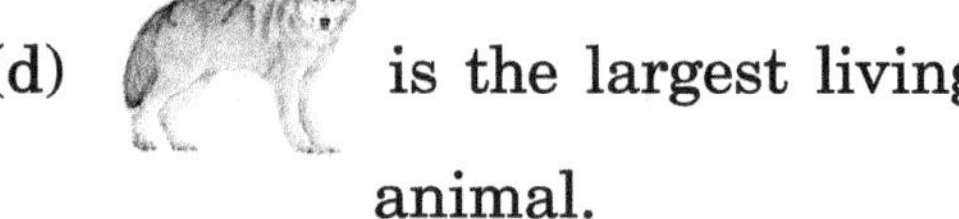 is the largest living animal.

16. Which part of our body helps us to hear a bell?

(a) Eye   (b) Nose

(c) Ear   (d) Tongue

17. The picture shows that our house keeps us safe from

(a) the heat of the Sun

(b) rain

(c) wild animals

(d) all of these

18. Choose the correct sequence of words to complete the paragraph given below.

Summer days are _______ while winter days are ______. A strong wind blows on _____ . Moonsoon days are ______.

(a) cold, hot, windy day, rainy

(b) rainy, cold, a hot day, windy

(c) hot, cold, a windy day, rainy

(d) windy, hot, a rainy day, cold

19. Consider the following two statements:

Statement A: Carpenter makes shoes.

Statement B: Plumber works in the post office.

Which of the following is correct with respect to the above statement?

(a) Statement A is correct.

(b) Statement B is correct.

(c) Statement A and B are correct.

(d) Neither statement A nor statement B is correct.

20. Which of the following is considered as a family member?

(a) Uncle

(b) Wife

(c) Teacher

(d) Both (a) & (b)

21. Which of the following fruits has only one seed?

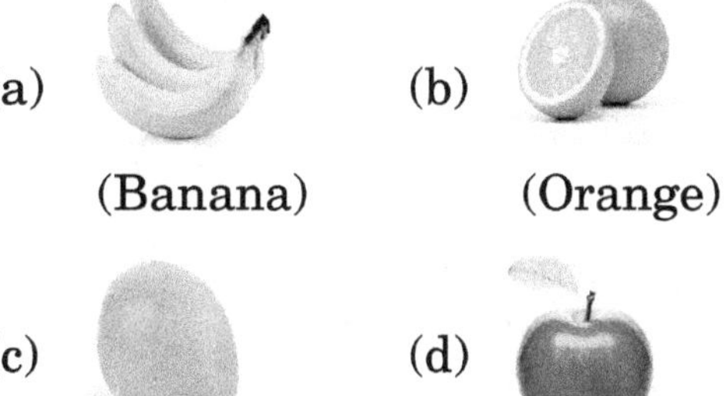

(a) (Banana) (b) (Orange)

(c) (Mango) (d) (Apple)

22. Find the odd one out.

(a) Desk (b) Scale

(c) Eraser (d) Tree

23. Consider the following two statements and choose the correct answer.

Statement A: Air does not have weight.

Statement B: Air is needed for burning.

(a) Statement A is true and Statement B is false.

(b) Statement B is true and Statement A is false.

(c) Both the statements are true.

(d) Both the statements are false.

24. Which of the following is true about food?

   A.   Food gives us energy.

   B.   Energy giving food also contains fats.

   C.   Milk is a complete food.

   D.   Food do not protect our body from diseases.

	A	B	C	D
(a)	1	2	3	4
(b)	2	4	3	1
(c)	3	4	2	1
(d)	4	3	2	1

  (a) A, B, D   (b) A, C, D

  (c) A, B, C   (d) A, B, C, D

25. Match the following.

List I		List II
A.	Eye	1.
B.	Nose	2.
C.	Hand	3.
D.	Teeth	4.

26. Match the following.

	List I		List II
A.	Shrub	1.	Ashok
B.	Tree	2.	Bean
C.	Climber	3.	Rose
D.	Creepers	4.	Pumpkin

	A	B	C	D
(a)	1	3	2	4
(b)	3	2	1	4
(c)	3	1	2	4
(d)	2	3	4	1

27. Doctors work in which of the following places?

(a) 
Hospital

(b) 
Post Office

(c) 
Police Station

(d)
Temple

28. Which of these is a national festival of India?

(a) 

(b) 

(c) 

(d)

29. Read the following sentences and choose True (T)/False(F).

1. Sun changes its shape every night.

2. Stars look very small because they are far from us.

3. Moon does not have its own light.

(a) TTF   (b) FTT

(c) TTT   (d) TFT

30. Which of the following modes of transport does not have engines and is not pulled by animals?

(a) 
Jeep

(b) 
Car

(c) 
Tonga

(d) 
Cycle

_______________ *Space for Rough Work* _______________

31. Tyres are made up of __________.

    (a) wood   (b) metal

    (c) rubber   (d) glass

32. Which of the following is man made?

    (a) 

    Mountains

    (b) 

    River

    (c) 

    Rocket

    (d) 

    Desert

33. Look at the picture carefully. If you were to see them again after 1 year, whose size would remain the same?

    (a) 

    Baby boy

    (b) 

    Puppy

    (c) 

    Small plant

    (d) 

    Toy Robot

Space for Rough Work

34. Let us assume that 'rain' is called 'water', 'water' is called 'sky' and 'sky' is called 'cloud'. Based on this, where would planes fly?

(a) Rain   (b) Water

(c) Cloud   (c) Sky

35. In the classification chart below, where would you put a shark ?

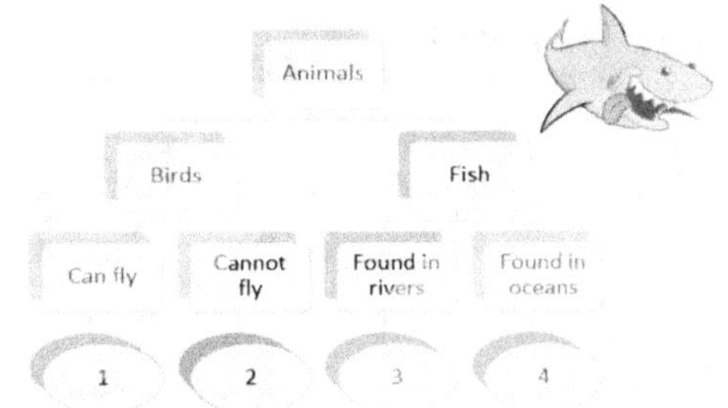

(a)   in place of 1
(b)   in place of 2
(c)   in place of 3
(d)   in place of 4

OLYMPIAD
Mock Test 2

Name : _______________

Number of Questions : 35

Max. Marks : 35

Time : 2 Hours

There is no negative marking in the test.

1. Which of the following is the national tree of India?

   (a) Mango tree

   (b) Coconut tree

   (c) Banyan tree

   (d) None of these

2. Solve the riddle.

   I catch thieves and make sure that everybody follow rules.
   Who I am?

   (a) Policeman (b) Carpenter

   (c) Milkman (d) Doctor

3. Which of the following is not a sense organ?

   (a) Nails

   (b) Teeth

   (c) Eye

   (d) Both (a) and (b)

4. Match the following.

	List I		List II
A.	Bus stop	1.	A path for walking
B.	Footpath	2.	A black and white path across a road
C.	Queue	3.	A place where bus regularly stop
D.	Zebra crossing	4.	A line of people

Space for Rough Work

	A	B	C	D
(a)	3	1	4	2
(b)	1	3	1	1
(c)	2	2	2	3
(d)	4	4	3	4

5. Which of the following does not help in building a house?

(a) Electrician (b) Plumber

(c) Policeman (d) Mason

6. Which of the following is a non-living thing which is used for travelling from one place to another?

(a) Horse   (b) Train

(c) Oxen   (d) Donkey

7. Which of the following birds cannot fly?

(a) Sparrow   (b) Pigeon

(c) Parrot   (d) Penguin

8. Which of the following vegetable is green in colour?

(a) Spinach

(b) Peas

(c) Carrot

(d) Both (a) and (b)

9. Which of the following is not made up of plastic?

(a) Bottle   (b) Blade

(c) Lunch Box (d) Pencil box

Space for Rough Work

10. Which of the following things we must do after and before eating food?

(a) Wash your hands

(b) Take a bath

(c) Take a proper sleep

(d) All of these

11. We like to sit near this when we feel hot.

(a) Bulb   (b) Heater

(c) Table fan   (d) Toaster

12. Which of the following is a family member?

(a) Uncle   (b) Nephew

(c) Aunt   (d) All of these

13. Identify the fruit.

(a) 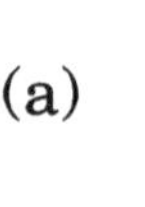   (b) 

Carrot   Tomato

(c)    (d) None of these

Cucumber

14. Match the following.

	List I		List II
A.	Leg	1.	Listen
B.	Skin	2.	Watch
C.	Ear	3.	Walk
D.	Eyes	4.	Feel

	A	B	C	D
(a)	1	1	4	1
(b)	2	2	2	3
(c)	3	4	1	2
(d)	4	3	3	4

15. What does the green colour say in traffic signal?

   (a) Wait   (b) Enjoy

   (c) Go   (d) Stop

16. Which of the following are used to prepare salad?

   (a) Tomato

   (b) Potato

   (c) Cucumber

   (d) Both (a) & (c)

17. Which of the following is a place of worship?

   (a) Temple   (b) Church

   (c) Mosque   (d) All of these

18. Who among the following persons stitches your clothes?

   (a) 

   (b) 

   (c) 

   (d) 

19. Identify the insects.

   (a)    (b) 

   (c)    (d) 

   (a) B   (b) B, C, D

   (c) B and D   (d) A, C, D

20. You are given a picture of an aquarium. Identify the non-living thing.

    (a) Fish

    (b) Water plants

    (c) Octopus

    (d) Stones

21. What is the common thing that is required for cooking, washing, bathing and planting a tree?

    (a) Air   (b) Sunlight

    (c) Water   (d) All of these

22. Which of the following protect us from rain?

    (a) Raincoat

    (b) Umbrella

    (c) Socks

    (d) Both (a) and (b)

23. Which of the following can move from one place to another?

    (a) Airport

    (b) Police Station

    (c) Bus

    (d) Mango tree

24. Consider the following statements.

    Statement A: Dolphin is a water plant.

    Statement B: Drinking water must be clean.

    Which of the following is correct with respect to the above statements?

Space for Rough Work

(a) Statement A is correct and statement B is wrong.

(b) Statement B is correct. and statement A is wrong.

(c) Statement A and B are correct.

(d) Neither statement A nor Statement B is correct.

25. Who works in a school?

(a) Nurse (b) Teacher

(c) Barber (d) Waiter

26. The ___________ takes care of the school garden.

(a) gardener (b) teacher

(c) milkman (d) all of these

27. When do we celebrate the birthday of Gandhi Ji?

(a) 2nd January

(b) 26 October

(c) 14 November

(d) 2nd October

28. Which of the following things are used to play holi?

(a) Crackers

(b) Gulal

(c) Coloured water

(d) Both (b) and (c)

29. Which of the following activities are dangerous?

(A) (B)

(C) (D)

(a) A (b) A, B, C, D

(c) B, C, D (d) A, B, C

Space for Rough Work

30. Which of the following is a body part?

    (a) Head

    (b) Head light

    (c) Headmaster

    (d) Headache

31. Which of the following is not present in pairs?

    (a) Nose   (b) Ears

    (c) Hands   (d) Legs

32. What would one normally not do in the kitchen of a house?

    (a) Wash and cut vegetables

    (b) Make a cup of coffee

    (c) Store all utensils

    (d) Brush our teeth

33. What is the common between all the animals shown in the picture?

    (a) They can all fly.

    (b) None of them can fly.

    (c) They all eat plants.

    (d) They are all birds.

34. The boy in the picture loves playing the detective. He wants to find out what is the girl's shirt made of.

    What did he see?

    (a) Jute   (b) Plastic

    (c) Thread   (d) Wire

35. Match the following.

List I   **List II**

A 

(1)   Furniture

B

(2)   Food grain

C

(3)   Fruit

D

(4)   Perfume

(a)   A-2, B-3, C-1, D-4   (b)   A-3, B-2, C-4, D-1

(c)   A-1, B-2, C-4, D-3   (d)   A-3, B-1, C-3, D-4

OLYMPIAD
Mock Test

Name : __________

Number of Questions : 35

Max. Marks : 35

Time : 2 Hours

There is no negative marking in the test.

1. Which of the following is the living thing?

    (a) Bag   (b) Neem Tree

    (c) Desk   (d) Pencil

2. Arrange the following sentences in correct order.

    I   Cut the fruits safely with knife.

    II   Clean your hands first.

    III Wash the fruits.

    IV   Eat the fruits as they keep us healthy.

    (a) I–II–III–IV (b) II–III–IV–I

    (c) IV–III–II–I (d) II–III–I–IV

3. Head : Brain :: Chest : __________

    (a) Bones   (b) Heart

    (c) Fingers   (d) Skin

4. Which of the following is not made up of plastic?

    (a) Chair   (b) Pencil box

    (c) Bottle   (d) Bulb

5. Which of the following items do we get from plants?

    (a) Wood   (b) Fruits

    (c) Pulses   (d) All of these

Space for Rough Work

6. Amit has two animals. They both are very useful to him. One gives milk and other is used for travelling from one place to another. Which of the following animals does Amit have?

   (a) Cow and lion

   (b) Goat and hen

   (c) Cow and horse

   (d) Cow and deer

7. Hat is used to protect which of the following parts of your body?

   (a) Knee   (b) Heart

   (c) Thumb   (d) Head

8. What is the common thing that a kite needs to fly as well as a person needs to breathe?

   (a) Air   (b) Rain

   (c) Food   (d) None of these

9. If 4 people want to move together from one place to another which of the following means of travel can be used?

   (a) Car   (b) Aeroplane

   (c) Cycle   (d) Train

10. Why we should not burn fire crackers on diwali?

    (a) They make air dirty.

    (b) They create lot of noise.

    (c) They are harmful for our health.

    (d) All of these

11. Who among the following helps you when you are with high fever and stomach pain?

    (a) Doctor   (b) Policeman

    (c) Milkman   (d) Tailor

12. Which of the following is the right way to board a school bus when you are standing in a line?

    (a) Wait for your turn.

    (b) Push others to board the bus first.

    (c) Keep waiting on the bus stand till next day to board bus first.

    (d) Stop going to school.

13. You should use _________ while washing dirty hands.

    (a) toothpaste

    (b) soap

    (c) milk

    (d) none of these

14. Which of the following is used in winters?

    (a) Cotton clothes

    (b) Woollen clothes

    (c) Rain coat

    (d) None of these

15. Which of the following animals, kids love to play with?

    (a) Dog

    (b) Rabbit

    (c) Giraffe

    (d) Both (a) and (b)

16. Which of the following is not a fruit?

    (a) Grapes

    (b) Watermelon

    (c) Cucumber

    (d) Orange

17. Which of the following is not true about plants?

    (a) They provide us food.

    (b) They can move from one place to another.

    (c) They are green in colour.

    (d) They need water to grow.

Space for Rough Work

18. Who makes your school uniform?

    (a) Tailor   (b) Barber

    (c) Carpenter   (d) Plumber

19. Which of the following first aids you would have given to your friend who got hurt while playing with you and his left arm is bleeding?

    (a) Gently rub his left arm.

    (b) Hold his left arm still.

    (c) Apply dettol to avoid infection.

    (d) Tell him to do some exercise.

20. Which of the following is the mother of your father?

    (a) Aunt

    (b) Grandmother

    (c) Maternal Aunt

    (d) Stranger

21. Human body is made up of different __________.

    (a) organs

    (b) sense organs

    (c) systems

    (d) all of these

22. I am a green-coloured bird. I eat green chilly. Who am I?

    (a) Parrot   (b) Sparrow

    (c) Crow   (d) Pigeon

23. Which of the following do not run on the roads?

    (a) Ship

    (b) Train

    (c) Scooter

    (d) Both (a) and (b)

—————————— *Space for Rough Work* ——————————

24. Which of the following is the most beautiful part of a plant?

    (a) Leaves

    (b) Flower

    (c) Stem

    (d) None of these

25. Which of the following animals lives in the forest?

    (a) Giraffe   (b) Tiger

    (c) Zebra   (d) All of these

26. Which of the following can be used to travel in air?

    (a) Car

    (b) Ship

    (c) Auto rickshaw

    (d) Aeroplane

27. Whom do we call neighbours?

    (a) People living near our house.

    (b) People living in sky.

    (c) People living in hospital.

    (d) People living far from our house.

28. How do you feel hot, cold, rough and smooth?

    (a) With your skin

    (b) With your legs

    (c) With your eyes

    (d) Both (b) and (c)

29. 

    Identify the festival in the given picture.

    (a) Eid   (b) Diwali

    (c) Holi   (d) None of these

———————— *Space for Rough Work* ————————

30. Which of the following birds can we keep at our home as a pet?

    (a) Peacock   (b) Parrot

    (c) Crow   (d) Eagle

31. Read the following sentences and choose the True(T)/False(F).

    1. Diwali is the festival of colours.

    2. Sewain is prepared on Eid.

    3. Gandhi Jayanti is a national festival.

    (a) TTF   (b) TFT

    (c) FTT   (d) TFF

32. In which of these seasons, weather is neither hot nor cold?

    (a) Spring   (b) Autumn

    (c) Winter   (d) Both (a) & (b)

33. Choose the odd one out.

    (a) Mud   (b) Straw

    (c) Brick   (d) Bamboo

34. Animals which eat only grass are

    (a) herbivores

    (b) carnivores

    (c) omnivores

    (d) none of these

35. Who lives in  (nest)?

    (a) 

    (b) 

    (c) 

    (d) None of these

Space for Rough Work

Name : __________

Number of Questions : 40

Max. Marks : 40

Time : 2 Hours

There is no negative marking in the test.

1. Which of the following comes from plants?

   (a) Tea (b) Coffee

   (c) Sugar (d) All of these

2. Consider the following two statements.

   Statement A: Bird is a living thing.

   Statement B: Water is a non-living thing.

   Which of the following is correct with respect to the above statement?

   (a) Statement A is correct.

   (b) Statement B is correct.

   (c) Statement A and B are correct.

   (d) Neither statement A nor statement B is correct.

3. Which of the following are water animals?

   (a) Dolphin

   (b) Blue Whale

   (c) Rabbit

   (d) Both (a) & (b)

4. Which of the following eats grass?

   (a) 
   Tiger

   (b) 
   Lion

   (c) 
   Rabbit

   (d) 
   Dog

Space for Rough Work

5. Which of the following is true about non-living things?

   A. Non-living things do not move.

   B. Non-living things never die.

   C. Non-living things do not breathe.

   D. Neem tree is a non-living thing.

   (a) A,B,C   (b) B,C,D

   (c) A,D   (d) C,D

6. Consider the following two statements.

   Statement A: Husband and wife are not family members.

   Statement B: Cousins are family members of a small family.

   (a) Statement A is correct.

   (b) Statement B is correct.

   (c) Statement A and B are correct.

   (d) Neither statement A nor statement B is correct.

7. Which of the following is true about post office?

   A. In post office we post our letters.

   B. We buy stamps.

   C. Maintains law and order.

   (a) A,C   (b) A,B

   (c) A,B,C   (d) B,C

8. Find the incorrect match.

   (a) Red-Wait
   (b) Yellow-Go
   (c) Green-Go
   (d) Wait-Yellow

—————————————— *Space for Rough Work* ——————————————

9. Do not play with _______.

(a) 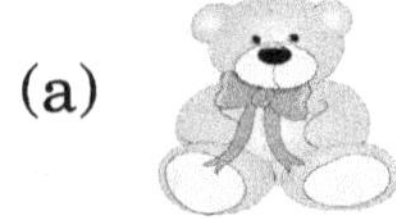 (b) 

(c)  (d) 

10. We take help of many people to make our life easy. Look at the picture and identify which of these persons helps us in this situation?

(Thief)

(a) Driver   (b) Nurse

(c) Chemist   (d) Police

11. Where do people live?

(a)  (b) 

Sun   Moon

(c)  (d)

Earth   Stars

12. Identify the personality:

(a) A. P. J. Abdul Kalam

(b) Mahatma Gandhi

(c) Albert Enstein

(d) Rabindranath Tagore

Space for Rough Work

13. Which of the following is the fastest and most expensive mods of transportation?

(a)  Aeroplane

(b)  Ship

(c)  Train

(d)  Car

14. Lalita is Kapil's grandmother and Raghav is Kapil's father. Then what is the relationship between Lalita and Raghav?

(a) Father - Son

(b) Mother - Son

(c) Brother - Sister

(d) Uncle - Neice

15.  are made up of which of the following material?

(a) Wood   (b) Glass

(c) Rubber   (d) None of these

16. Things shown below are found in

(a) kitchen

(b) bedroom

(c) drawing room

(d) balcony

17. Which animal feeds on dead animals?

(a) Vulture

(b) Elephant

(c) Cow

(d) None of these

———————— Space for Rough Work ————————

18. Tick the animal which lay eggs?

(a) 

(b) 

(c) 

(d) None of these

19. Match the following.

List (i)		List (ii)	
(A)		(1)	Glass
(B)		(2)	Rubber
(C)		(3)	Wood
(D)		(4)	Leather

	A	B	C	D
(a)	1	2	4	3
(b)	3	1	4	2
(c)	2	1	3	4
(d)	1	4	3	2

20. Which of the following sense organs are involved in the following situation?

A. A boy listening music.

B. A boy watching a bird in the sky.

C. A girl eating ice cream.

(a) Ear, Skin, Tongue

(b) Ear, Eye, Tongue

(c) Eye, Ear, Skin

(d) Ear, Eye, Nose

21. Your Uncle Sam is living in Australia with his family. It is not possible to meet them daily. Which of the following is the best way to communicate with them?

    (a) E-mail

    (b) Mobile phone

    (c) Post Card

    (d) Both (a) & (b)

22. Which of the following can be eaten only after cooking?

    (a) Radish   (b) Brinjal

    (c) Carrot   (d) Apple

23. Consider the following statements and choose the correct answer.

    Statement A : Brain is an excretory organ.

    Statement B: Heart supplies blood to the body.

    (a) Statement A is true, statement B is false.

    (b) Statement B is true, statement A is false.

    (c) Both the statements are true.

    (d) Both the statements are false.

24. Very small plants are called _______.

    (a) herbs   (b) climbers

    (c) leaves   (d) creepers

25. Which of the following is are an insect?

    (a) Mosquito

    (b) Ant

    (c) Parrot

    (d) Both (a) & (b)

Space for Rough Work

26. Identify the non-living thing.

27. Which of the following have very weak stem and need support to grow?

(a) Herbs   (b) Shrubs

(c) Climbers   (d) Trees

28. Which of the following sense organs helps us to smell?

(a) Eye   (b) Ear

(c) Nose   (d) Hands

29. Consider the following two statements.

Statement A: Tiger is a domestic animal.

Statement B: Frog is not a domestic animal.

Which of the following is true with respect to the above statement?

(a) Statement A is true and statement B is false

(b) Statement B is true and statement A is false

(c) Both the statements are true.

(d) Both the statements are false.

30. Which of the following statements is true?

(a) Pineapple is a vegetable.

(b) Pumpkin is a vegetable.

(c) Wheat is a vegetable.

(d) Guava is a vegetable.

—————————————— *Space for Rough Work* ——————————————

31. Select the incorrect match.

    (a)   Lion - den

    (b)   Bird - nest

    (c)   Dog - kennel

    (d)   Horse - burrow

32. Which of the following statements is true?

    (a)   Raincoat is used in winter.

    (b)   Sweater is used in winter.

    (c)   Raincoat is used in monsoon.

    (d)   Both (b) & (c)

33. What do you mean by water conservation?

    (a)   Using excessive water

    (b)   Reducing the use of water

    (c)   Drinking more water

    (d)   Not using water

34. Which of the following statements is true?

    (a)   Sun can produce heat and light of their own.

    (b)   Sun is a star.

    (c)   Moon does not has its own light.

    (d)   All of these

35. What will you call the mother of your father?

    (a)   Aunt

    (b)   Sister

    (c)   Grandmother

    (d)   Niece

36. Which of the following animals eat insects?

    (a)    (b) 

    (c)    (d) 

Space for Rough Work

37. Which sense organ helps us to read a book?

    (a) Eye   (b) Ear

    (c) Nose   (d) Skin

38. This keeps our bones and teeth strong?

    (a)    (b) 

       Cucumber   Watermelon

    (c)    (d) 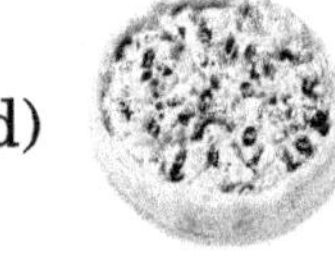

        Milk   Pizza

39. For lighting a  we need ———.

    (a) air

    (b) water

    (c) food

    (d) all of these

40. On a cold day, we like to have this?

    (a) Lemonade   (b) Ice cream

    (c) Hot coffee   (d) Popcorn

OLYMPIAD
Mock Test

Name : __________

Number of Questions : 40

Max. Marks : 40

Time : 2 Hours

There is no negative marking in the test.

1. Find the odd one out.

   (a) Temple

   (b) School

   (c) Gurudwara

   (d) Mosque

2. Which of the following will you find in forest, jumping on the trees?

   (a) Monkey

   (b) Deer

   (c) Tiger

   (d) Cow

3. Which of the following is a non-living thing?

   (a) Car

   (b) Bus

   (c) Horse

   (d) Both (a) & (b)

4. Which of the following needs air to breathe?

   (a) Football   (b) Balloon

   (c) Cat   (d) All of these

5. Choose the odd one out.

   (a) Human   (b) Animal

   (c) Food   (d) Plant

—————————— *Space for Rough Work* ——————————

6. Look at the picture and identify the personality:

(a) Mother Teresa

(b) Mahatma Ganhdi

(c) Jawaharlal Nehru

(d) Dr. A. P. J. Abdul Kalam

7. Choose the odd one out.

(a) Heater   (b) Sweater

(c) Gloves   (d) Skirt

8. Christmas : Christians : : Republic day : _________

(a) Indians

(b) Muslims

(c) Sikh

(d) None of these

9. Which of the following is a good habit?

A. Use shower for bathing.

B. Do not close taps after use.

(a) Both A and B are true

(b) Only A is true

(c) Only B is true

(d) Both (A) and (B) are false

10. Match the phrases with the given words.

List I		List II	
A.	Peacock	1.	Water animal
B.	Octopus	2.	Bird
C.	Insect	3.	Animal
D.	Sheep	4.	Fly

	A	B	C	D
(a)	2	1	4	3
(b)	1	2	3	1
(c)	3	3	1	4
(d)	4	4	2	2

———— Space for Rough Work ————

11. Children of uncles and aunts are called ________.

    (a) friends   (b) daughters

    (c) neighbours (d) cousins

12. Which of the following in not true about the food we eat?

    (a) All living things need food to survive.

    (b) Food helps us to grow.

    (c) Foods are obtained from plant as well as animals.

    (d) Food makes us weak and unhealthy.

13. Which part of your body is red in colour?

    (a) Tongue   (b) Hair

    (c) Eyes   (d) Teeth

14. Match the following.

	List I		List II
A.	Mango Tree	1.	Made up of wood
B.	Table	2.	Energy giving thing
C.	Milk	3.	Non-living thing
D.	Doll	4.	Living thing

	A	B	C	D
(a)	1	4	3	2
(b)	2	1	4	3
(c)	3	1	4	2
(d)	4	1	2	3

15. Which of the following is needed by a human body to grow?

    (a) Doll   (b) Milk

    (c) Books   (d) Watch

Space for Rough Work

16. Never touch electric switches and plugs with ______. It may give you an electric shock.

    (a) empty hands

    (b) wet hands

    (c) full hands

    (d) dry hand

17. Fallen leaves are ________.

    (a) living things

    (b) non-living things

    (c) both (a) & (b)

    (d) none of these

18. Which of the following is an external part of the human body?

    (a) Heart   (b) Brain

    (c) Lungs   (d) Nose

19. Which of the following is used by villagers to travel from one place to another?

    (a) Helicopter

    (b) Bullock Carts

    (c) Cars

    (d) Boats

20. Which of the following is a family occasion?

    (a)

    (b)

    (c)

    (d) Both (b) & (c)

21. Which of the following you do not see usually in your neighbourhood?

(a) Parks   (b) Schools

(c) Airports   (d) Markets

22. Which of the following is an incorrect match?

(a) Fireman : sells milk

(b) Cobbler : mends shoes

(c) Postman : brings letters

(d) Carpenters : makes furniture

23. Which of the following is used to make "Chapatti" ?

(a) 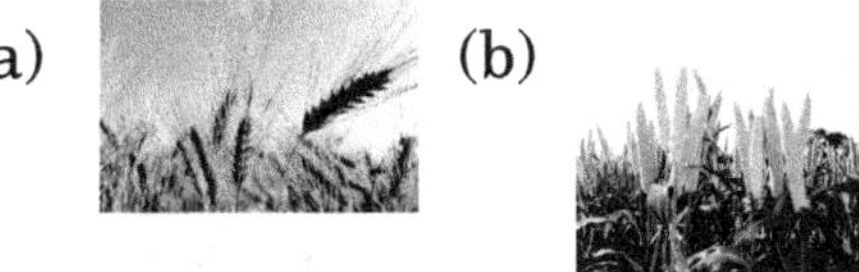   (b)

(c)    (d) None of these

24. Which of the following is NOT considered as a good habit?

(a) Keep books in their right place.

(b) Exercise daily.

(c) Eat healthy food daily.

(d) Lick fingers after eating.

25. After it rains, we see a ______ in the sky.

(a) rainfall   (b) rainbow

(c) rainbird   (d) rainsky

26. Which of the following is NOT used to describe the weather?

(a) windy   (b) rainy

(c) hot   (d) sweet

Space for Rough Work

27. Which of the following we do not get from plants?

    (a) Mango   (b) Milk

    (c) Rice   (d) Carrot

28. Match the following.

	List I		List II
A.	Butterfly	1.	Flightless bird
B.	Penguine	2.	Large animal
C.	Elephant	3.	Pet animal
D.	Cat	4.	Fly in air

	A	B	C	D
(a)	4	1	2	3
(b)	2	2	3	2
(c)	3	3	4	4
(d)	1	4	1	1

29. Flowers change into __________.

    (a) fruits   (b) plants

    (c) dry fruits   (d) water

30. What is the common thing that a ship, fish and a plant needs?

    (a) Petrol   (b) Water

    (c) Leaves   (d) Fruits

31. You have to go to your friend's birthday party but you want to change your hairstyle. Who will help you to get a new hairstyle?

    (a) Barber   (b) Teacher

    (c) Tailor   (d) Cobbler

Space for Rough Work

32. Which of the following one should keep in mind before crossing the road?

    (a) Look left and right before crossing the road.

    (b) Eat banana before crossing the road

    (c) Drink some water and take a deep breath.

    (d) All of these

33. Ram and Rohan have same mother, Mrs. Geeta. What do you think is the relation between Ram and Rohan?

    (a) Brothers

    (b) Cousins

    (c) Friends

    (d) Neighbours

34. Look at the pictures and tell what is the common thing used in both the picture?

FIG - 1   FIG - 2

    (a) Cooking gas

    (b) Food

    (c) Water

    (d) Bucket

35. The meal which we eat in the afternoon is called_____.

    (a) nutrition   (b) lunch

    (c) Dinner   (d) breakfast

Space for Rough Work

36. _______ grow crops in the field.

   (a) Doctor

   (b) Cobbler

   (c) Farmer

   (d) Driver

37. A kutcha house is mostly found in the _______.

   (a) cities   (b) town

   (c) villages   (d) both (a) and (b)

38. Which of these is celebrated by all Indians?

   (a) Gandhi Jayanti

   (b) Diwali

   (c) Eid

   (d) Holi

39. Which of the following eats flesh of dead animals?

   (a) Pigeon   (b) Vulture

   (c) Horse   (d) Parrot

40. Select the INCORRECT pair of animal and its home.

   (a) Squirrel-Tree holes

   (b) Owl-Nest

   (c) Lion-Den

   (d) Horse-Stable

GENERAL KNOWLEDGE MOCK TEST 1–5

OLYMPIAD
Mock Test 1

Name : __________

Number of Questions : 25

There is no negative marking in the test.

Max. Marks : 25

Time : 1 Hour

Section I
General Awareness

1. We go to ______________ to buy medicines.

   (a) dairy

   (b) pharmacy

   (c) bakery

   (d) grocery shop

2. A person who travels to space is called a/an ______________.

   (a) astronaut (b) cobbler

   (c) blacksmith (d) dentist

3. Which festival is depicted in the image given below?

   (a) Diwali   (b) Dussehra

   (c) Holi   (d) Lohri

4. Identify 'Gateway of India' in the images given below.

   (a)    (b) 

   (c)    (d) 

Space for Rough Work

5. Which of the following is the national animal of India?

(a) 

(b) 

(c) 

(d) 

6. Which of the following images shows a place of worship called 'Gurudwara'?

(a) 

(b) 

(c) 

(d) 

7. Identify national flower of India in the images given below.

(a) 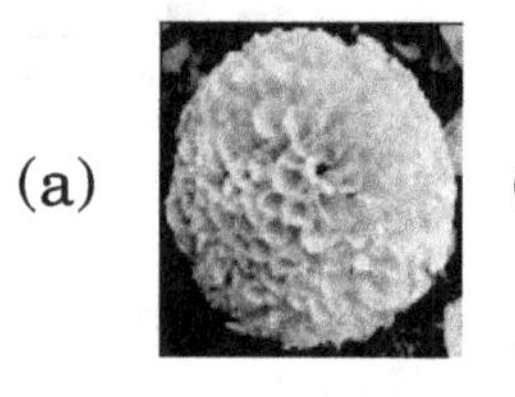

(b) 

(c) 

(d) 

8. Which of the following persons is also known as 'Father of the Nation'?

(a) 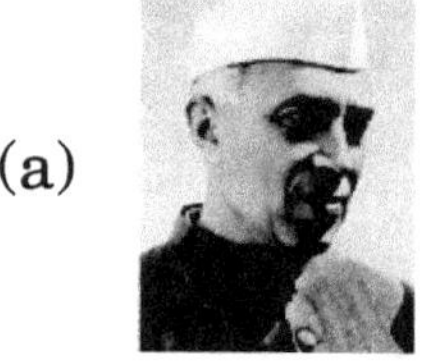

(b) 

(c) 

(d) 

9. Which of the following is the longest river in India?

   (a) Ganga   (b) Yamuna
   (c) Brahmaputra   (d) Jhelum

10. Animals which live in water are called _____________________.

   (a) land animals

   (b) aquatic animals

   (c) aerial animals

   (d) none of these

11. Who was the first president of India?

   (a) Dr. Rajendra Prasad

   (b) Zakir Husain

   (c) V.V. Giri

   (d) Gyani Jail Singh

12. With which sports is 'P.V. Sindhu' associated?

   (a) Cricket   (b) Football
   (c) Badminton   (d) Hockey

13. Which of the following is NOT a pet animal?

   (a)   (b)

   (c)   (d)

14. Which of the following is not a farm animal?

   (a) Cow   (b) Pig
   (c) Lion   (d) Hen

15. In which city is the Red Fort situated?

   (a) Agra   (b) Lucknow
   (c) Delhi   (d) Chandigarh

16. _______ is the capital city of India.

   (a) Kolkata

   (b) New Delhi

   (c) Mumbai

   (d) Bangaluru

—————————— *Space for Rough Work* ——————————

17. Which of the following numbers has five tens and seven ones?

    (a) 507   (b) 57

    (c) 75   (d) 571

18. Which of the following toys is the costliest?

    (a)   ₹ 189.09   (b)   ₹ 189.99

    (c)   ₹ 179.89   (d)   ₹ 189.95

19. Currently who is the captain of Indian cricket team?

    (a)    (b) 

    (c)    (d) 

20. Who among the following has been recently elected as 14th president of India?

    (a) 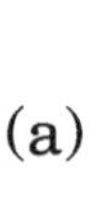    (b) 

    (c)   (d)  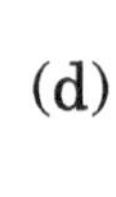 

21. Which cartoon character becomes strong by eating spinach?

    (a) Tom   (b) Popeye

    (c) Shinchan   (d) Doremon

22. One of your classmates has stolen your pencil box, you should

    (a) keep it a secret.

    (b) tell your teacher.

    (c) engage in a fight.

    (d) buy a new pencil box.

23. What is the first thing you need to do, if you want to wash your clothes?

    (a) Clean the washing machine.

    (b) Sort your clothes by colour and fabric.

    (c) Wash your hands.

    (d) Switch on the washing machine.

Section II
Achievers Section

24. Match items in column I with column II and choose the correct answer from given options.

Column I	Column II
A. Gandhi Jayanti	(i) 14th November
B. Republic Day	(ii) 15th August
C. Children's Day	(iii) 2nd October
D. Independence Day	(iv) 26th January

    (a) A-i, B-iii, C-iv, D-ii

    (b) A-iv, B-i, C-ii, D-iii

    (c) A-iii, B-iv, C-i, D-ii

    (d) A-iii, B-ii, C-iv, D-i

25. Animals that eat meat are called ____________.

    (a) farm animals

    (b) carnivores

    (c) herbivores

    (d) mammals

—————— Space for Rough Work ——————

OLYMPIAD
Mock Test 2

Name : _________

Number of Questions : 25

Max. Marks : 25

Time : 1 Hour

There is no negative marking in the test.

Section I
General Awareness

1. Which of the following is NOT a national festival?
   (a) Gandhi Jayanti
   (b) Independence Day
   (c) Christmas
   (d) Republic Day

2. Which festival is the image given below associated with?

   (a) Christmas
   (b) Holi
   (c) Onam
   (d) Raksha Bandhan

3. Who among the following is also known as 'Bapu'?

   (a) 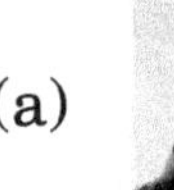  (b) 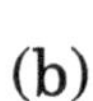 

   (c)  (d) 

4. Which of the following is NOT related to computers?

   (a) Mouse   (b) Pen

   (c) Monitor   (d) Keyboard

5. Which of the following fruits is also the name of a reputed computer company?

   (a) apple   (b) grapes

   (c) mango   (d) banana

6. Gurupurab is celebrated by ________.

   (a) Muslims   (b) Sikhs

   (c) Hindus   (d) Christians

7. Which community helper do you see in a hospital?

   (a) Carpenter (b) Nurse

   (c) Plumber   (d) Blacksmith

8. Which of the following community helpers make iron tools?

   (a) Carpenter (b) Cobbler

   (c) Plumber   (d) Blacksmith

9. How will you relate to your maternal grandfather?

   (a) Your father's father

   (b) Your mother's father

   (c) Your father's grandfather

   (d) None of these

10. Which of the following is NOT a river?

   (a) Ganga   (b) Kaveri

   (c) Everest   (d) Yamuna

11. Which sport is Mary Kom related with?

   (a) Cricket   (b) Tennis

   (c) Boxing   (d) Chess

12. Who wrote the national song of our country?

   (a) Bankim Chandra Chatterji

   (b) Rabindranath Tagore

   (c) Swami Vivekanand

   (d) Vinoba Bhave

Space for Rough Work

13. Who was the first president of India?

(a)    (b)

(c)    (d)

14. The baby of a frog is called _________________.

    (a) calf   (b) fawn

    (c) tadpole   (d) larva

15. A horse lives in a ______________.

    (a) sty   (b) shed

    (c) den   (d) stable

16. We wear ___________ to keep our hands warm in the winter.

    (a) muffler   (b) bangles

    (c) socks   (d) gloves

17. Mother of a calf is ______________.

(a)    (b)

(c)    (d)

18. Who brings your letter home from the post office?

    (a) Doctor   (b) Gardener

    (c) Postman   (d) Mother

19. Which dog is Mickey Mouse's pet?

    (a) Scooby Doo (b) Pluto

    (c) Snowy   (d) Snoopy

20. Who is the current president of India?

    (a) Pranab Mukharjee

    (b) A.P.J. Abdul Kalam

    (c) M. Venkaiah Naidu

    (d) Ram Nath Kovind

———————————— Space for Rough Work ————————————

21. If you want to call police in case of an emergency, which number will you dial?

(a) 500   (b) 100
(c) 110   (d) 200

22. Which of the following is NOT a type of bird?

(a) Penguin   (b) Crow

(c) Chimpanzee (d) Ostrich

23. Which of the following things cannot be observed at night?

(a) Sun   (b) Moon

(c) Star   (d) Meteorite

Section II
Achievers Section

24. How many states are there in India ?

(a) 26   (b) 27

(c) 28   (d) 29

25. ________________ is the smallest country in the world.

(a) Vatican City (b) Maldives

(c) Sri Lanka   (d) Singapore

OLYMPIAD
Mock Test 3

Name : _____________

Number of Questions : 25

There is no negative marking in the test.

Max. Marks : 25

Time : 1 Hour

Section I
General Awareness

1. Which vaccine is given free of cost every month to all children below 5 years?
   (a) Polio (b) Dengue
   (c) BCG (d) Hepatitis

2. Which animal is called ship of the desert?

   (a) 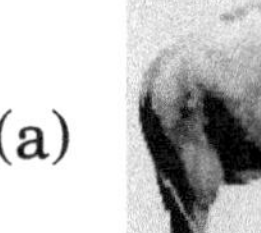 (b) 

   (c)  (d) 

3. Which is the shortest month of the year?
   (a) December (b) May
   (c) February (d) October

4. Which is the official language of India ?
   (a) Hindi (b) English
   (c) Punjabi (d) Telgu

5. Which is the largest animal in the world?
   (a) Blue whale
   (b) African elephant
   (c) Giraffe
   (d) Rhino

Space for Rough Work

6. Which is the largest continent in the world?

   (a) Asia   (b) Europe

   (c) Africa   (d) Australia

7. One hundred years make a _______________.

   (a) century   (b) millennium

   (c) decade   (d) none of these

8. The monument shown in the image below is situated in _______________.

   (a) Ahmedabad

   (b) New Delhi

   (c) Mumbai

   (d) Bengaluru

9. A _______________ is a type of computer which can be carried from one place to another.

   (a) laptop   (b) desktop

   (c) smartphone (d) none of these

10. _______________ is the largest country in the world.

   (a) England   (c) China

   (c) Australia   (d) Russia

11. _______________ is a special dish made during Eid-ul-Fitr.

   (a) Seviyan   (b) Gujhiya

   (c) Kheer   (d) Halwa

12. How many days are there in the month of February in a leap year?

   (a) 28   (b) 29

   (c) 30   (d) 31

13. Which of the following festivals celebrates the victory of good over evil?

   (a) Christmas (b) Dussehra

   (c) Onam   (d) Janamashtmi

14. Christmas is celebrated on _______________.

   (a) 26th January

   (b) 15th August

   (c) 25th December

   (d) 2nd October

Space for Rough Work

15. Which of the following is a domestic animal?

(a)  (b) 

(c)  (d) 

16. A/an _________________ carries many people to far off places.

(a) car (b) bus

(c) aeroplane (d) boat

17. Which bird runs very fast but cannot fly?

(a)  (b) 

(c)  (d) 

18. Which of the following is a type of bird that lives in very cold region?

(a) 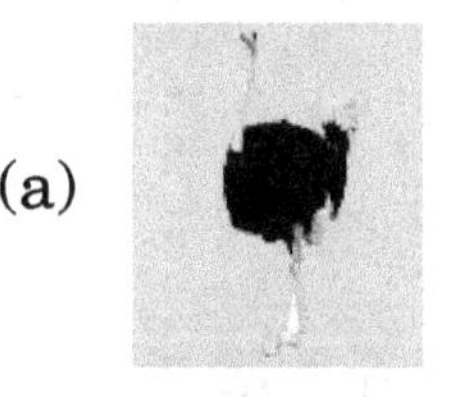 (b) 

(c)  (d) 

19. Who is known as 'Big B'?

(a) (b) 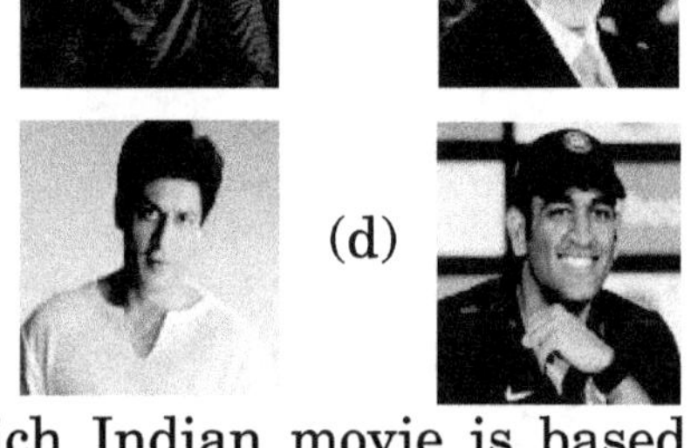

(c) (d)

20. Which Indian movie is based on the life of a hockey player?

(a) Dangal (b) Three Idiots

(c) Gold (d) Sultan

Space for Rough Work

21. Currently who is the president of United States of America?

(a)    (b) 

(c)    (d) 

22. Which of the following vehicles has a siren?

(a)    (b) 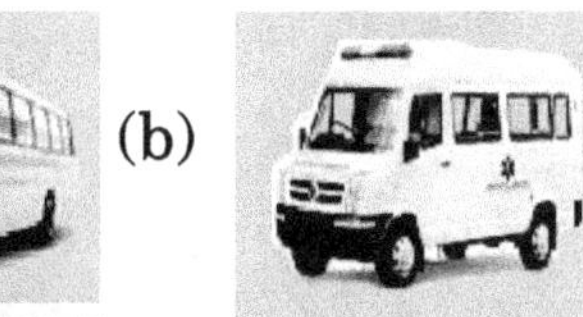

(c)    (d) 

23. The food which gives us energy is

(a)    (b) 

(c)    (d) 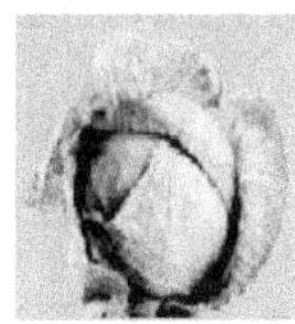

Section II
Achievers Section

24. Which of the following planets is also called the blue planet?

(a) Jupiter   (b) Earth

(c) Mercury   (d) Venus

25. Match the states with their capitals and choose the correct answer from given options.

States	Capitals
A. Gujarat	(i) Lucknow
B. Rajasthan	(ii) Mumbai
C. Uttar Pradesh	(iii) Gandhinagar
D. Maharashtra	(iv) Jaipur

(a) A-i   B-iii   C-iv   D-ii

(b) A-iv   B-i   C-ii   D-iii

(c) A-iii   B-iv   C-i   D-ii

(d) A-iii   B-ii   C-iv   D-i

Space for Rough Work

Name : __________

Number of Questions : 40

Max. Marks : 40

Time : 2 Hours

There is no negative marking in the test.

Section I
General Awareness

1. Which of the following insects makes honey?

(a) 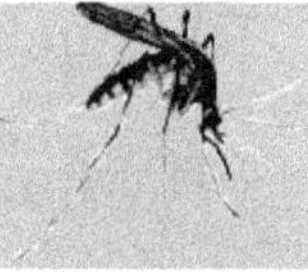 (b) 

(c)  (d) 

2. Which among the following animals has a horn on its nose?
   (a) Hippopotamus
   (b) Rhinoceros
   (c) Elephant
   (d) Giraffe

3. The animal which does not have legs is ____________.
   (a) frog   (b) porcupine
   (c) monkey   (d) snake

4. Baby of a goat is called _________.
   (a) calf   (b) lamb
   (c) kid   (d) cub

5. Baby of a deer is called _________.
   (a) kid   (b) fawn
   (c) infant   (d) calf

6. The lion lives in a _____________.
   (a) shed   (b) house
   (c) den   (d) nest

Space for Rough Work

7. Pick the odd one out.

(a)  (b) 

(c)  (d) 

8. Baby of a kangaroo is called
    _______________________________.

    (a) calf   (b) cub

    (c) leveret   (d) joey

9. The dog lives in a _______________.

    (a) kennel   (b) cave

    (c) nest   (d) burrow

10. Which sound does a pig make?

    (a) Trumpet   (b) Oink

    (c) Quack   (d) Chirp

11. Which of the following is the hottest planet?

    (a) Mercury   (b) Venus

    (c) Earth   (d) Mars

12. Which of the following is the largest planet?

    (a) Earth   (b) Mars

    (c) Jupiter   (d) Neptune

13. Which of the following sports persons is called the 'Master Blaster'?

(a)  (b) 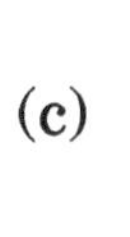

(c)  (d) 

14. Which of the following sports persons is called the 'Flying Sikh'?

    (a) Bishan Singh Bedi

    (b) Milkha Singh

    (c) Harbhajan Singh

    (d) Dhyan Chand

15. What sports is played at Wimbledon?

(a)  (b)

(c) (d)

16. How many spokes does the wheel in the Indian flag have?

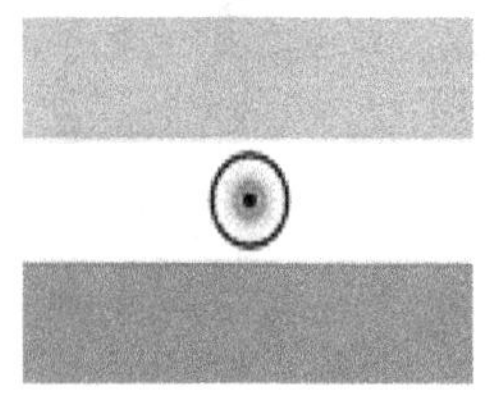

(a) 10   (b) 20
(c) 24   (d) 28

17. Who wrote the National Anthem of India?

(a) Subhash Chandra Bose

(b) Rabindranath Tagore

(c) Bankim Chandra Chatterji

(d) Womesh Chander Banerjee

18. Who was the 1st Prime Minister of India?

(a) 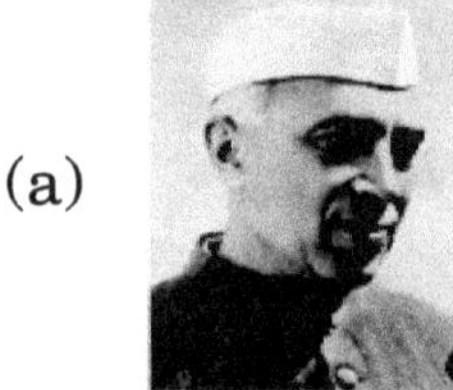 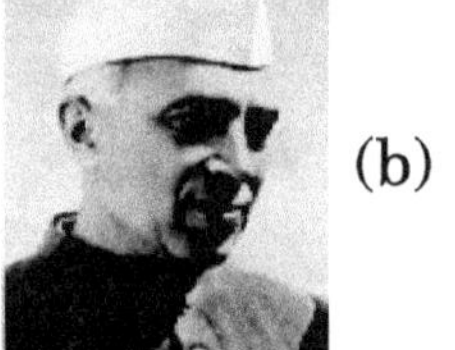 (b) 

(c) 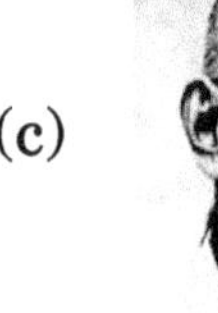  (d) 

19. Who is known as the Nightingale of India?

(a) Indira Gandhi

(b) Sarojini Naidu

(c) Lata Mangeshkar

(d) Asha Bhonsale

20. What comes out of the egg of a butterfly?

(a) Tadpole   (b) Caterpillar

(c) Earthworm   (d) Ladybird

--------- *Space for Rough Work* ---------

21. Name the 3 main body parts of a butterfly.

    (a) Head, Thorax, Abdomen

    (b) Antennae, Head, Legs

    (c) Front, Middle, Back

    (d) Antennae, Body, Legs

22. How many legs do butterflies have?

    (a) 2   (b) 4

    (c) 6   (d) 8

23. Which of the following is the nearest star to planet Earth?

    (a) Sun   (b) North Star

    (c) Pole star   (d) Sirius

24. Which of the following is not a sense organ of our body?

    (a) Nose   (b) Skin

    (c) Eyes   (d) Legs

25. Which of the following is the fastest animal on the land?

(a)    (b) 

(c)    (d) 

26. Which of the following is the most sensitive part of our body?

    (a) Skin   (b) Tooth

    (c) Hair   (d) Nail

27. Which of the following is the most eco-friendly source of energy?

    (a) Solar power (b) Wood

    (c) Coal   (d) Petrol

28. What are the two holes in the nose called?

    (a) Nostrils   (b) Elbows

    (c) Ankles   (d) Heels

_______________________ *Space for Rough Work* _______________________

29. Which of the following is the longest river on the earth?

   (a) Nile   (b) Ganges

   (c) Rhine   (d) Amazon

30. Which of the following fruits gives us oil?

   (a)   (b)

   (c)   (d)

31. Which of the following is a fruit?

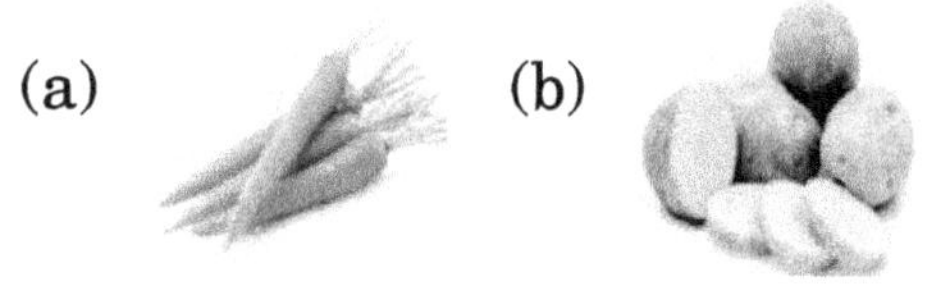

   (a)   (b)

   (c)   (d)

32. The hard part inside our body is called _________________.

   (a) skin   (b) bone

   (c) tissue   (d) muscle

33. Most widely spoken language in the world is _________________.

   (a) Hindi   (b) English

   (c) Spanish   (d) Chinese

34. Bhangra is the folk dance of _____________________.

   (a) Punjab

   (b) Assam

   (c) Gujarat

   (d) Andhra Pradesh

35. _________________ is the National tree of India

   (a) Peepal   (b) Banyan

   (c) Neem   (d) Tulsi

Space for Rough Work

36. Who among the following was popularly known as Netaji?

    (a) Vallabbhai Patel

    (b) Bal Gangadhar Tilak

    (c) Jawaharlal Nehru

    (d) Subhash Chandra Bose

Section II

Achievers Section

37. Who among the following Disney princesses was poisoned by an apple?

    (a) Cinderella

    (b) Snow white

    (c) Sleeping Beauty

    (d) Bella

38. Which of the following colours is not found in a rainbow?

    (a) Violet   (b) Yellow

    (c) Silver   (d) Orange

39. The baby of a zebra is called ___________________.

    (a) joey   (b) kitten

    (c) colt   (d) cub

40. Choose the most appropriate word to fill the blank.

    It _________ raining yesterday.

    (a) is   (b) was

    (c) were   (d) has

Space for Rough Work

OLYMPIAD
Mock Test 5 —

Name : __________

Number of Questions : 40

Max. Marks : 40

Time : 2 Hours

There is no negative marking in the test.

Section I
General Awareness

1. Which of the following is the smallest bird in the world?
   (a) Hummingbird
   (b) Parrot
   (c) Peacock
   (d) Sparrow

2. Which of the following is the tallest animal in the world?

   (a)  (b) 

   (c)  (d) 

3. Which of the following is the largest bird in the world?

   (a)  (b) 

   (c)  (d) 

4. What is an igloo made up of?
   (a) Cement   (b) Soil
   (c) Ice   (d) Straw

5. How many vowels are there in English alphabet?
   (a) 3   (b) 4
   (c) 7   (d) 5

———— Space for Rough Work ————

6. Which of the following planets has rings?

   (a) Earth   (b) Mars

   (c) Venus   (d) Saturn

7. Which of the following is the fastest moving planet?

   (a) Mars   (b) Mercury

   (c) Earth   (d) Jupiter

8. Which of the following is the largest desert in the world?

   (a) Thar desert

   (b) Kalahari desert

   (c) Arabian desert

   (d) Sahara desert

9. Which of the following is the largest ocean in the world?

   (a) Indian ocean

   (b) Atlantic ocean

   (c) Pacific ocean

   (d) Arctic ocean

10. Which of the following is the highest mountain peak in the world?

    (a) Kanchenjunga

    (b) Mount Everest

    (c) Nanda Devi

    (d) Mount Kilimanjaro

11. Which of the following countries is called 'Land of the Rising Sun'?

    (a) South Korea

    (b) New Zealand

    (c) Japan

    (d) Indonesia

12. Who built Taj Mahal at Agra?

    (a) Akbar   (b) Shahjahan

    (c) Jahangir   (d) Babur

13. In which season do we wear warm clothes?

    (a) Autumn   (b) Spring

    (c) Winter   (d) Summer

14. What is the shape of an egg?

    (a) Circle   (b) Oval

    (c) Sphere   (d) Round

———————————— *Space for Rough Work* ————————————

15. How many days are there in a leap year?

   (a) 364 days   (b) 365 days

   (c) 366 days   (d) 367 days

16. Which of the following body parts are not found in pairs?

   (a) Mouth   (b) Hands

   (c) Ears   (d) Eyebrows

17. Which of the following is the place of worship for Muslims?

   (a) 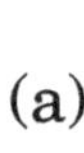    (b)

   (c) 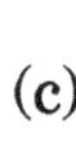    (d)

18. Baby of a horse is called ___________________.

   (a) calf   (b) colt

   (c) cub   (d) kitten

19. How many colours are there in our national flag?

   (a) Two   (b) Three

   (c) Four   (d) Five

20. Who was the first person to land on moon?

   (a) Yuri Gagrin

   (b) Denis Tito

   (c) Alexei Leonov

   (d) Neil Armstrong

21. Teacher's Day is celebrated on ___________________.

   (a) 5th September

   (b) 2nd October

   (c) 14th November

   (d) 10th December

22. Which of the following is the national bird of New Zealand?

   (a) Kiwi   (b) Peacock

   (c) Eagle   (d) Parrot

Space for Rough Work

23. Which of the following is equal to 500 paise?

(a)   (b) 

(c)    (d) 

24. A person who plays music is called a ___________________.

(a) singer   (b) musician

(c) composer   (d) dancer

25. What is full form of P.T.O.?

(a) Please Take Over

(b) Please Tick Out

(c) Please Turn On

(d) Please Turn Over

26. Gir National Park in Gujarat is famous for _______________

(a)    (b) 

(c) 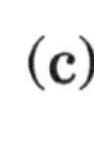   (d) 

27. Which of the following are built to control flood?

(a) Roads   (b) Bridges

(c) Dams   (d) Canals

28. How many letters are there in English alphabet?

(a) 24   (b) 25

(c) 26   (d) 27

29. Cataract is a disease of ___________________.

(a) ears   (b) lungs

(c) eyes   (d) heart

30. Which of the following animals has hump on its back?

(a) Horse   (b) Camel

(c) Elephant   (d) Giraffe

31. How many bones are there in our body?

(a) 200   (b) 206

(c) 210   (d) 220

32. How many teeth does an adult human have?

(a) 30   (b) 32

(c) 34   (d) 36

Space for Rough Work

33. How many players are there in a hockey team?

(a) 6   (b) 8

(c) 9   (d) 11

34. Which of the following plants grows in desert?

(a) 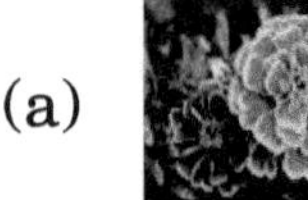   (b) 

(c)    (d) 

35. Which of the following is made from milk?

(a) 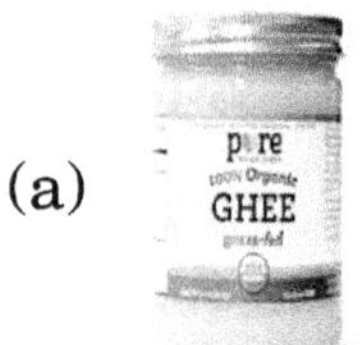   (b) 

(c)    (d) 

Section II
Achievers Section

36. Which of the following is different from the other three?

(a)    (b) 

(c) 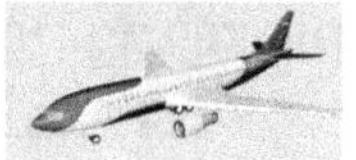   (d)

37. A figure with 3 sides is called a ___________________.

(a) square   (b) triangle

(c) rectangle   (d) circle

38. Agra is situated on the bank of river ___________________.

(a) Ganga   (b) Yamuna

(c) Narmada   (d) Gomti

39. A place where fish are kept is called a/an _________.

(a) aviary   (b) aquarium

(c) park   (d) zoo

40. Internet is used for _____________.

(a) e-mail   (b) chatting

(c) surfing   (d) all of these

Space for Rough Work

LOGICAL REASONING

MOCK TEST 1-5

Mock Test

Name : _____________

Number of Questions : 30

Max. Marks : 30

Time : 2 Hours

There is no negative marking in the test.

1. If **4** is related to ▲▲▲, then **5** is related to _____________.

    (a)

    (b) ▲▲

    (c)

    (d) ▲▲

2. If ◯△ is to △◯, then ⬢ is to _____________.

    (a)

    (b) ⬢

    (c) ⬢⬢

    (d) ⬢

3. ⬆⬇ : ⬆⬇ :: ⮕⬅ : ?

    (a) ⬆⬇

    (b) ⬆⬇

    (c) ⬅⮕

    (d) ⮕⬅

4. Share 8 muffins equally among 4 children.

    Each child gets _________ muffins.

(a) 3   (b) 4

(c) 2   (d) 8

5. Select the figure which is same as the given Fig. (X).

Fig. (X)

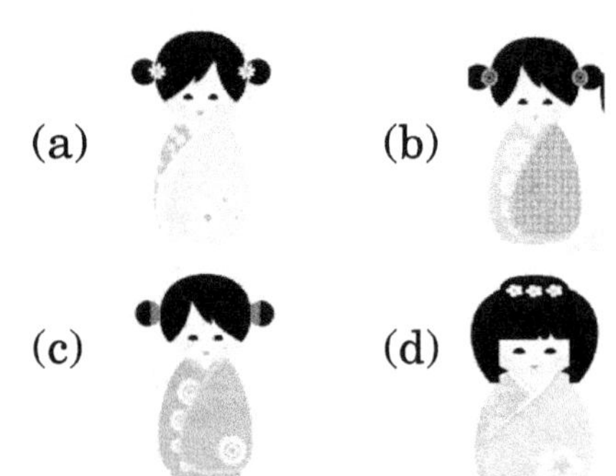

(a)   (b)

(c)   (d)

6. Which animal is in the first position?

(a) Lion   (b) Monkey

(c) Rabbit   (d) Elephant

7. There are three kittens. How many ears are there?

(a) 3   (b) 4

(c) 6   (d) 8

8. How much heavier is the book than the pencil ?

Use ⬤ as 1 unit

(a) 4 units   (b) 5 units

(c) 6 units   (d) 10 units

9. _______apples are inside the circle and _______ apples are outside the circle.

_____________ *Space for Rough Work* _____________

   (a) 3, 1   (b) 3, 3

   (c) 3, 2   (d) 2, 3

10. How many circles have two parts?

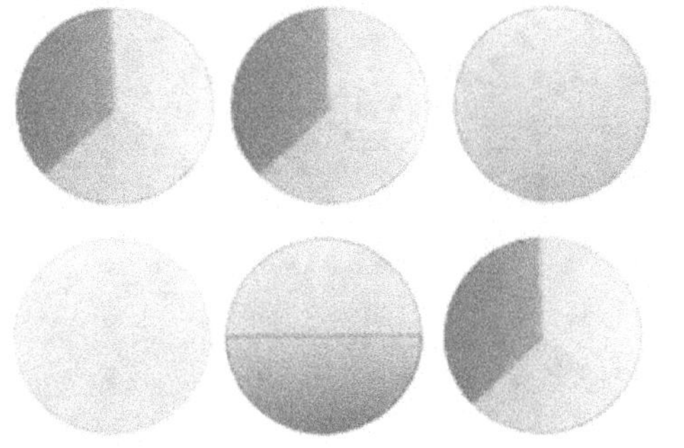

   (a) 2   (b) 3

   (c) 4   (d) 1

11. Which figure is greatest in number?

   (a) Square

(b) Circle

(c) Star

(d) Triangle

12. How many squares are there?

   (a) 7   (b) 6

   (c) 5   (d) 8

13. How many toffees will there be in the last box ?

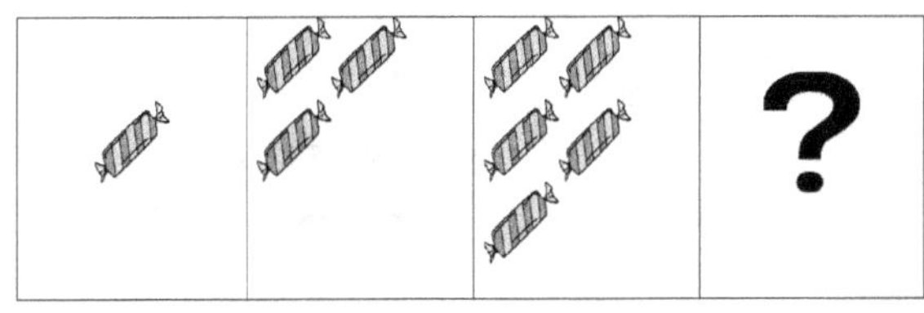

   (a) 6   (b) 7

   (c) 8   (d) 9

14. Identify the odd one out.

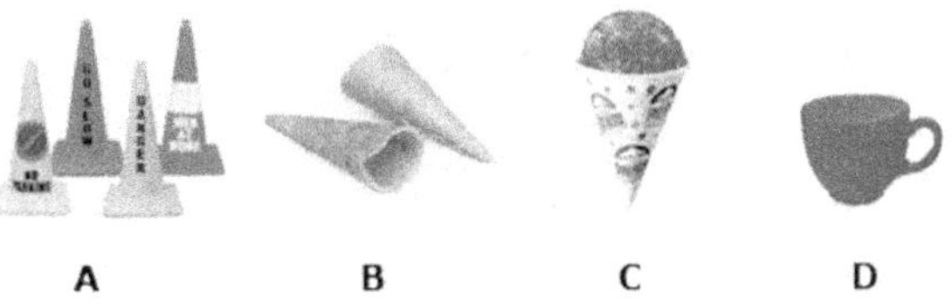

(a) A   (b) B

(c) C   (d) D

15. Complete the number pattern below.

The missing number is __________.

(a) 23   (b) 27

(c) 24   (d) 20

16. Look at the picture below. Choose all the things that have the shape of a rectangle.

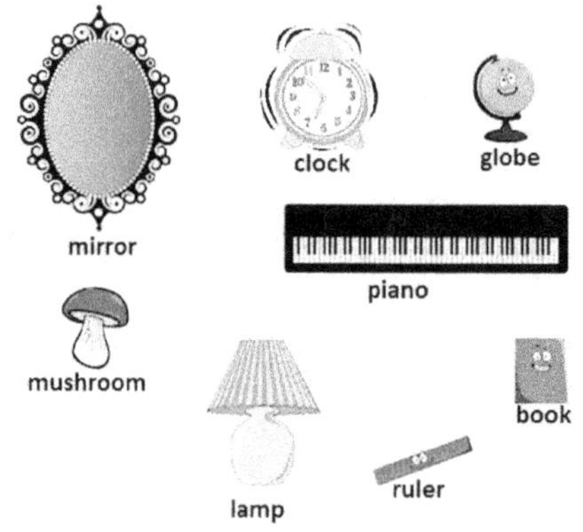

(a) Ruler and book

(b) Clock and globe

(c) Mushroom and mirror

(d) Piano, ruler and book

17. Myra wants to buy fourth flower from left. Which flower does she want ?

(a)   (b)

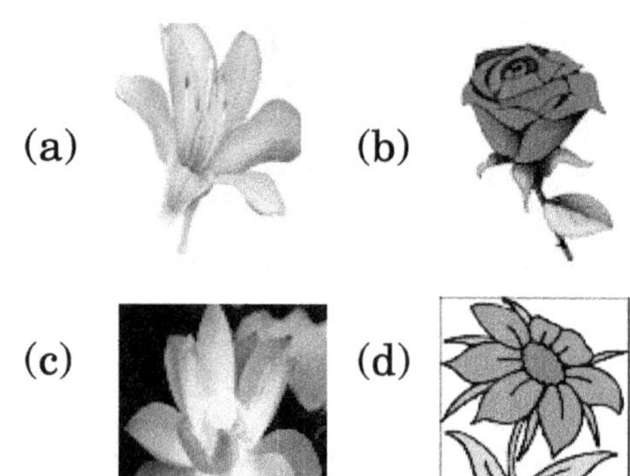

(c)   (d)

18. Name the animal that comes before lion from right end.

(a) Horse   (b) Zebra

(c) Cow   (d) Tortoise

Space for Rough Work

19.

(a) 5　　　　(b) 7

(c) 8　　　　(d) 10

20. Look at the picture carefully and answer the question.

Tower P is higher than Tower _____ but lower than Tower Q.

(a) Q

(b) R

(c) S

(d) None of these

21. Which squares are of the same size?

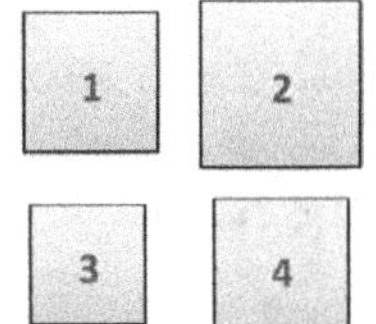

(a) 2 and 4　　　(b) 3 and 4

(c) 1 and 4　　　(d) 1 and 3

22. Complete the figure pattern shown below.

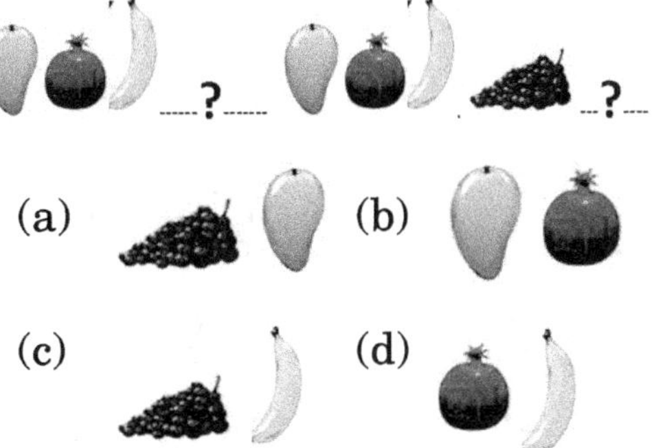

(a)　　　　(b)

(c)　　　　(d)

23. The picture shows the rectangular floor plan of the first level of a house?

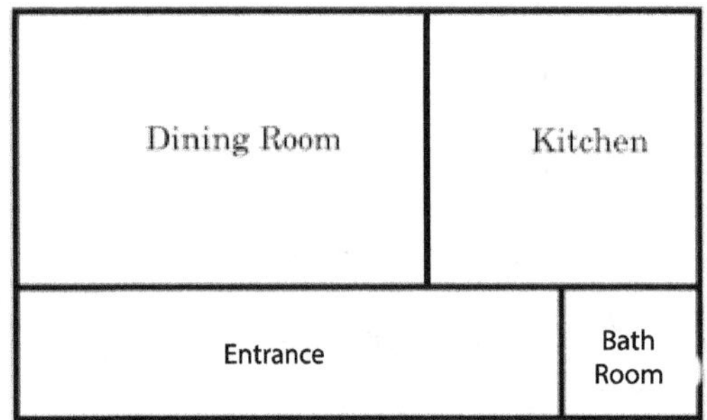

Which is the smallest room?

(a) Dining Room

(b) Kitchen

(c) Entrance

(d) Bathroom

24. How many bricks do you see?

(a) 7   (b) 6

(c) 5   (d) 4

25. 14 litres of water can be poured into which of the following pails? The capacity of each pail is given below.

(a) 6 ltrs pail   (b) 8 ltrs pail

(c) 12 ltrs pail   (d) 16 ltrs pail

26. Jyoti was 5 years old 2 years ago. How old is she now?

(a) 5 years old   (b) 6 years old

(c) 7 years old   (d) 8 years old

27. Rahul, Atul and Vikas are sitting in a row. Atul and Vikas are sitting at the ends. Who is sitting in the middle?

(a) Rahul   (b) Atul

(c) Vikas   (d) None of these

Space for Rough Work

28. Look at the picture below.

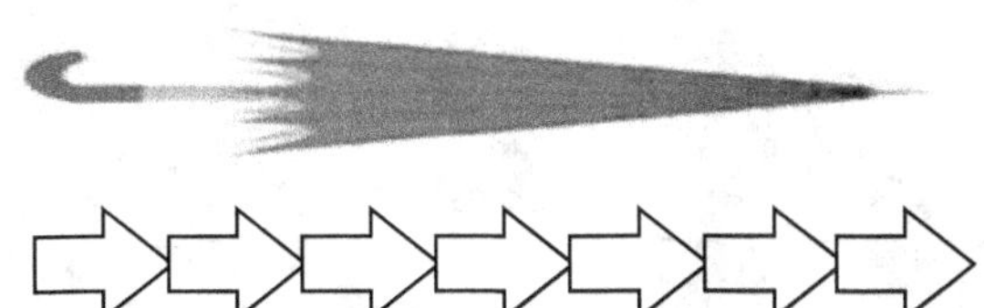

The length of the umbrella is about _________ ⇨ long.

(a) 6

(b) 7

(c) 5

(d) 8

29. Look at the following table.

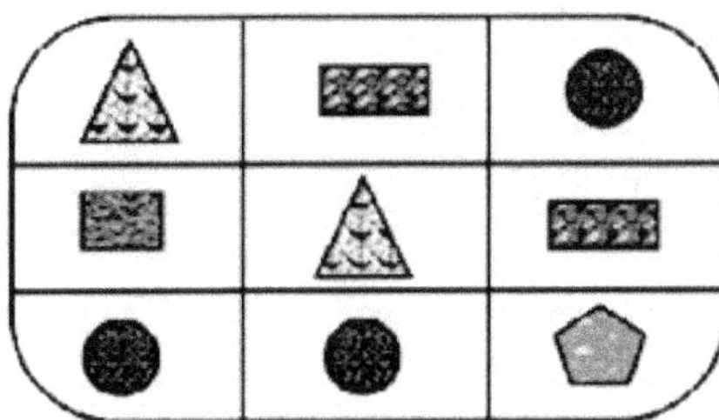

Which figure is in the centre of the table?

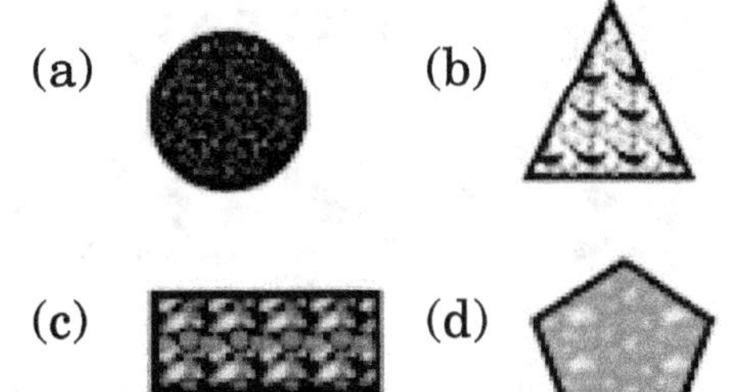

(a)

(b)

(c)

(d)

30. How many circles and triangles are below the red line?

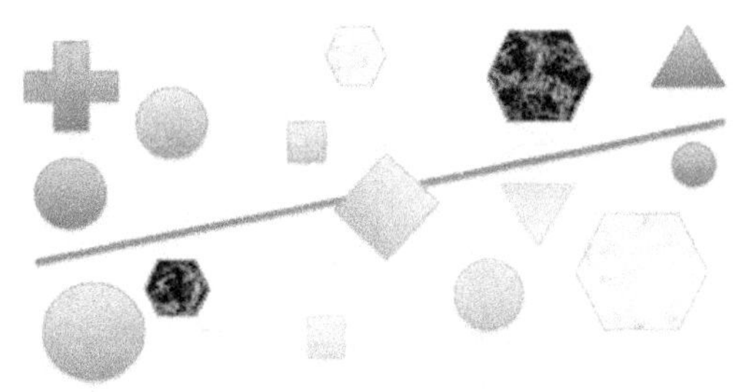

(a) 1

(b) 2

(c) 3

(d) 4

Name : __________

Max. Marks : 30

Number of Questions : 30

Time : 2 Hours

There is no negative marking in the test.

1. Find the missing shape in the given matrix.

   (a) hexagon
   (b) triangle
   (c) circle
   (d) rectangle

2. Complete the given figure.

   (a)
   (b)
   (c)
   (d)

3. Tape C is shorter than Tape D by _____ units.

   Each ⌷ stands for 1 unit.

   (a) 2
   (b) 3
   (c) 1
   (d) 4

4. How many matchsticks form a square?

(a) 3　　　　　　(b) 4

(c) 5　　　　　　(d) 6

5. Find out the odd one out.

(a) 　　　　(b) 

(c) 　　　　(d) 

Directions (Qs. 6 & 7): Study the given figure and answer the following questions.

6. ________ is standing nearest to the principal's room door.

(a) Rohan　　　(b) Naksh

(c) Ansh　　　(d) Ashima

7. ________ is standing farthest from the principal's room door.

(a) Rohan　　　(b) Naksh

(c) Ansh　　　(d) Priya

8. How many flowers are inside the vase?

(a) 4　　　　　　(b) 8

(c) 6　　　　　　(d) 5

Directions (Qs. 9 to 11): Choose the right answer.

---

9. The shape ◣ can be placed in which group?

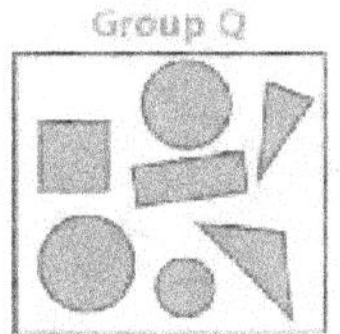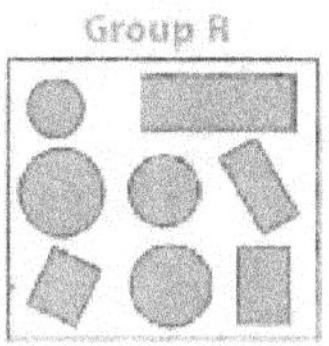

Space for Rough Work

(a) R and Q   (b) P and R

(c) P and Q   (d) P, Q and R

10. There are _______ groups of 2 ants.

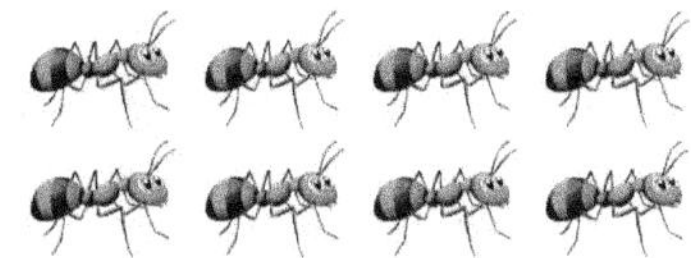

(a) 2   (b) 1
(c) 4   (d) 3

11. 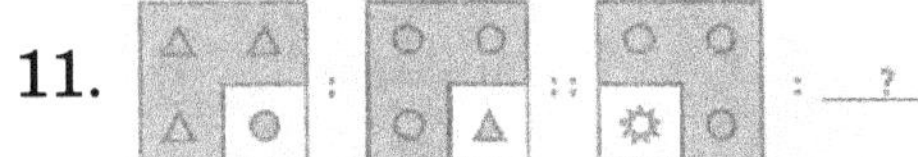

(a) 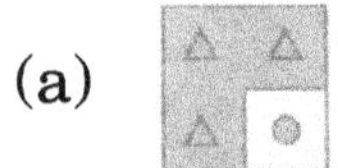   (b) 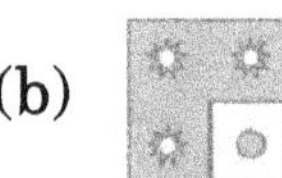

(c) 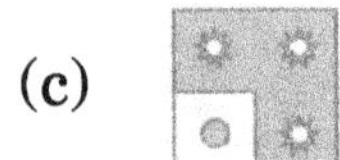   (d) 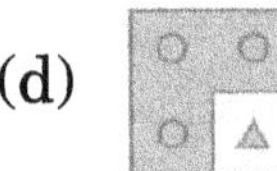

Directions (Qs. 12 & 13): Fill in the blanks.

12. Tom is just before _______ .

(a) Beena   (b) Latika

(c) Mohan   (d) Raghu

13. Raju is just after _______ .

(a) Raghu   (b) Megha

(c) Tom   (d) Garima

14. The 7th gift box from the right end is _______ .

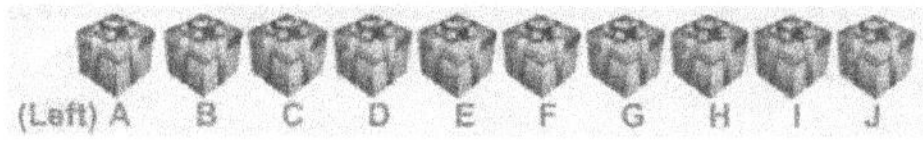

(a) G   (b) B

(c) D   (d) A

15. If  is to 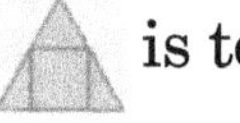 , then 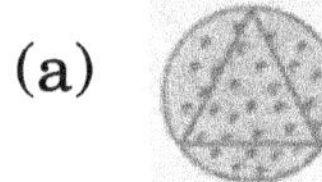 is to _______

(a) 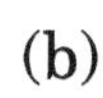   (b) 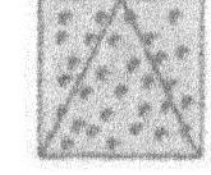

(c) 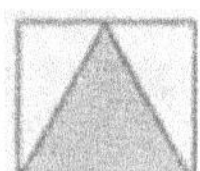   (d) 

Space for Rough Work

16. How many horses will have 8 legs?

   (a) 2   (b) 3

   (c) 4   (d) 5

17. How many  are there in box?

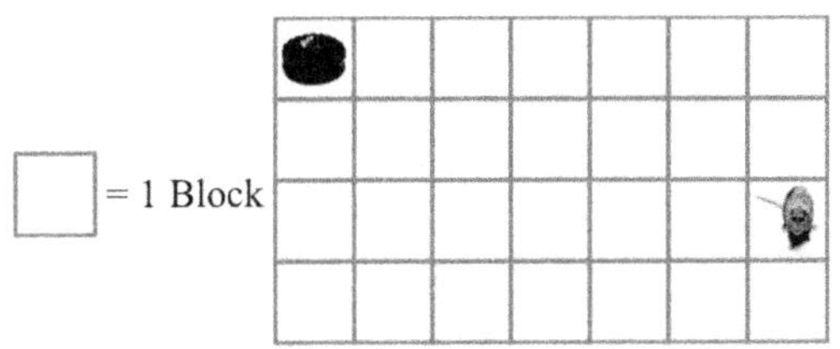

   (a) 22   (b) 23

   (c) 19   (d) 21

18. Minimum number of blocks a mouse runs to reach the cake, if it moves only in horizontal and vertical direction, is _______.

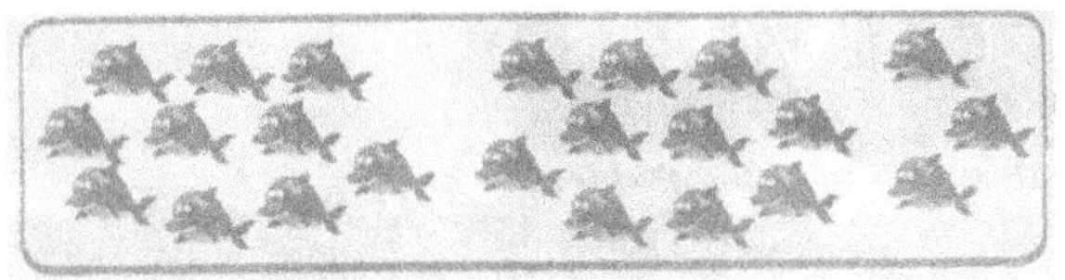

   (a) 9   (b) 8

   (c) 10   (d) 7

19. Which item is the heaviest ?

   (a)    (b) 

   (c)   (d)

20. How many such shapes are needed to form a circle?

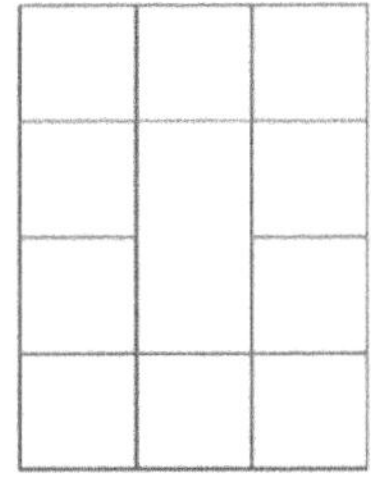

   (a) 2   (b) 3

   (c) 4   (d) None of these

21. How many small squares are there?

   (a) Eight squares

   (b) Nine squares

   (c) Ten squares

   (d) Twelve squares

Space for Rough Work

22. 

(a)    (b) 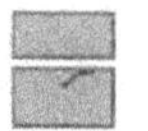

(c)    (d)

23. If there is no lamp in the picture, then the chair will be the _____ item from the left end.

(a) 5th   (b) 4th

(c) 3rd   (d) 2nd

24. How many squares are there in the figure?

(a) 12   (b) 14

(c) 15   (d) 17

25. Which toy is lightest?

(a) 

(b) 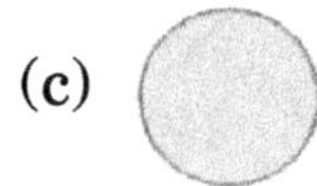

(c) 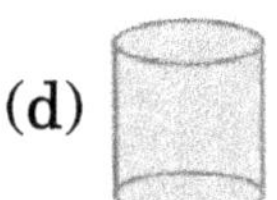

(d) Can't be determined

26. Find the odd one out.

(a)   (b)

(c)   (d)

27. Mukul, Raghav and Aryan are eating fruits on a hot summer day. Mukul and Raghav do not like to eat grapes. Who likes to eat grapes?

Space for Rough Work

(a) Mukul   (b) Raghav

(c) Aryan   (d) None

28. Three kids are standing in line waiting for the ice cream shop to open. Raj is standing in the middle. Nancy is standing directly behind Raj. Aanya is before Raj What is the correct order of line ?

(a) Aanya, Nancy, Raj

(b) Nancy, Aanya, Raj

(c) Aanya, Raj, Nancy

(d) None of these

29. Match the shapes in column I to the objects in column II which can be drawn with shapes in column I.

Column I   Column II

(A) 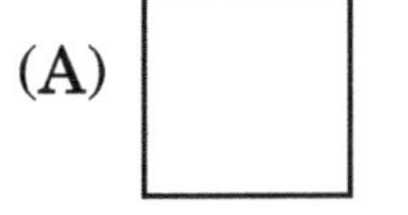   (i) 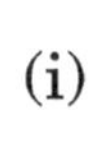

(B)    (ii) 

(C) ◯   (iii) 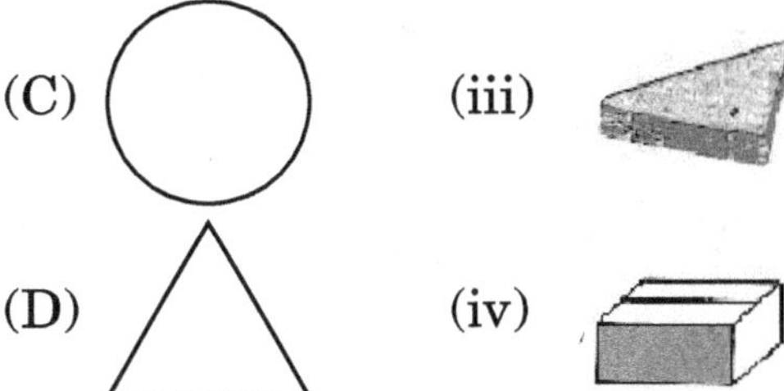

(D) △   (iv) 

(a) (A)-(iv), (B)-(ii), (C)-(i), (D)-(iii)

(b) (A)-(ii), (B)-(i), (C)-(iii), (D)-(iv)

(c) (A)-(ii), (B)-(iv), (C)-(i), (D)-(iii)

(d) (A)-(iii), (B)-(ii), (C)-(iv), (D)-(i)

30. Ten children are playing in the yard. There are 6 girls. How many boys are there ?

(a) Three   (b) Four

(c) Six   (d) Five

OLYMPIAD
Mock Test 3

Name : __________

Number of Questions : 30

Max. Marks : 30

Time : 2 Hours

There is no negative marking in the test.

1. Complete the figure pattern given below.

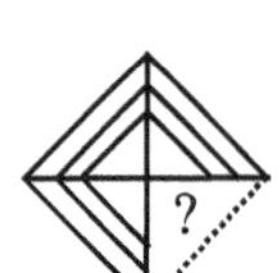

(a) 

(b) 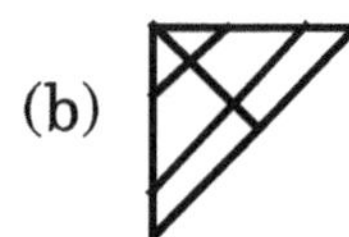

(c) 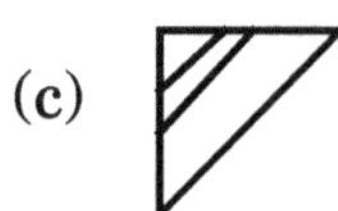

(d) 

2. Choose the correct option to replace the '?' mark.

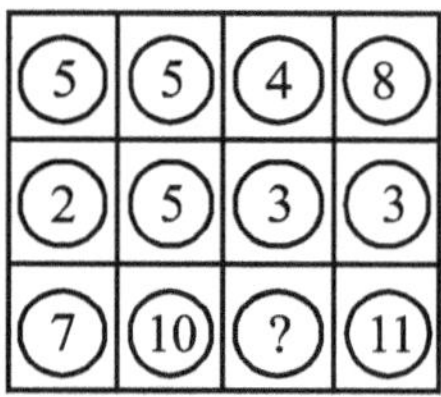

(a) 5   (b) 7

(c) 4   (d) 3

3. Four friends are standing together. ________ is the tallest and ______ is the shortest.

(a) P, Q   (b) S, R

(c) S, P   (d) Q, R

Space for Rough Work

4. The heaviest fruit is the _______ and lightest fruit is _______.

(a) banana and watermelon

(b) apple and banana

(c) watermelon and apple

(d) can't be determined

5. Anuj wakes up in the _________.

(a) morning (b) night

(c) evening (d) afternoon

Directions (Qs. 6 to 8): Study the given figure and answer the following questions.

6. There are _______ triangles.

(a) 6 (b) 5

(c) 8 (d) 9

7. There are _______ squares.

(a) 2 (b) 4

(c) 5 (d) 1

8. There are _______ circles and triangles altogether.

(a) 9 (b) 14

(c) 10 (d) 13

Space for Rough Work

Directions (Qs. 9 to 11): Find the odd one out.

9. (a) 

   (b) 

   (c) 

   (d) 

10. (a) 

   (b) 

   (c) 

   (d) 

11. (a) 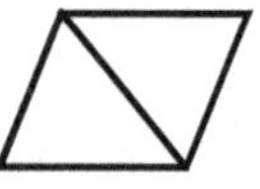   (b) 

   (c)    (d)

Directions (Qs. 12 & 13): Study the given figure carefully and answer the following questions.

12. _____ is running nearest to the finished line.

   (a) Sushma   (b) Satish

   (c) Rajiv   (d) John

13. _____ is running farthest from the finishing line.

   (a) Ajit   (b) Satish

   (c) Pramod   (d) Rahul

14. How many bananas are kept outside the basket?

(a) 4   (b) 3

(c) 5   (d) 6

15. There are _____ groups of 5 stars.

(a) 5   (b) 2

(c) 4   (d) 3

16. There are 6 equal groups of ___ cards.

(a) 3   (b) 6

(c) 2   (d) 4

17. How many balls are there in 2 equal groups of balls?

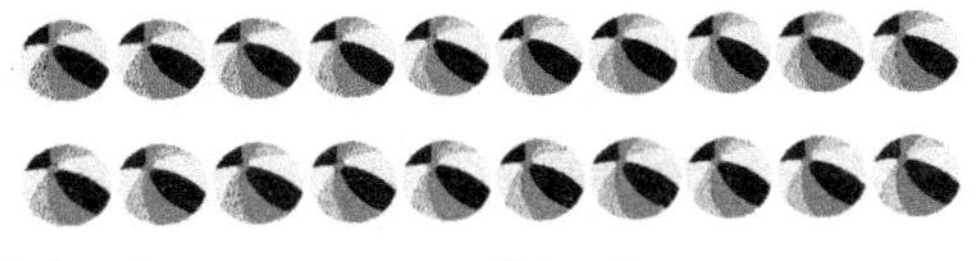

(a) 3   (b) 6

(c) 10   (d) 5

Directions (Qs. 18 to 20): There is a certain relationship between the pair of figures given on either side of : : . Identify the relationship of given pair and find the missing term.

18. 

(a)    (b) 

(c)    (d) 

19. 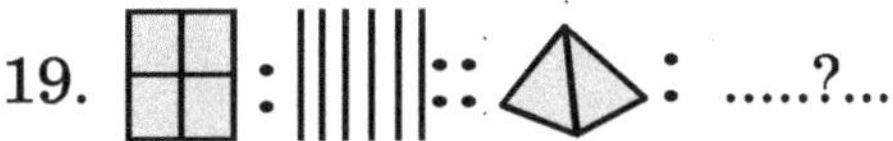

(a) |||| (b) ≡

(c) ||||| (d) ||||||

20.  :  :: 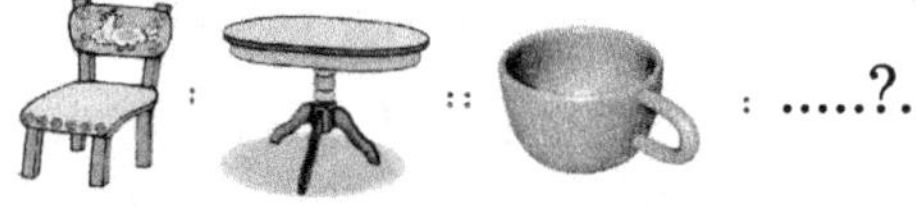 : .....?....

(a)   (b)

(c)   (d)

Directions (Qs. 21 & 22): Fill in the blanks.

21. Lakita is between ______ and ______.

(a) Deepak, Garima

(b) Ankit, Rahul

(c) Sahil, Arun

(d) Deepak, Ankit

22. Rahul is climbing just after ____.

(a) Ankit   (b) Deepak

(c) Latika   (d) Garima

23. The pencil that is 2nd from the left end is _______.

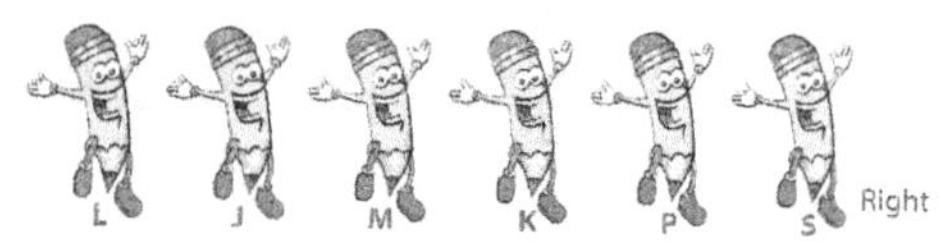

(a) J   (b) P

(c) M   (d) K

24. How many cubes are there?

(a) 4   (b) 5

(c) 6   (d) 7

Space for Rough Work

25. How many white squares are there?

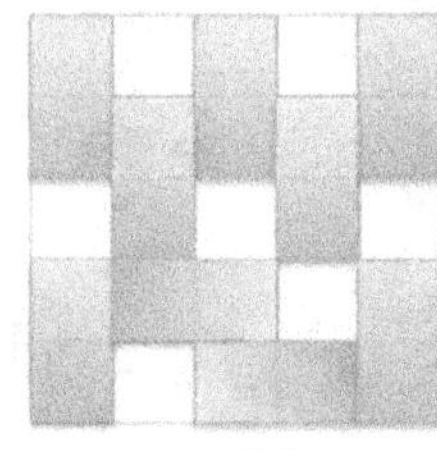

(a) 4   (b) 5

(c) 6   (d) 7

26. How many squares of the same size are there in the picture?

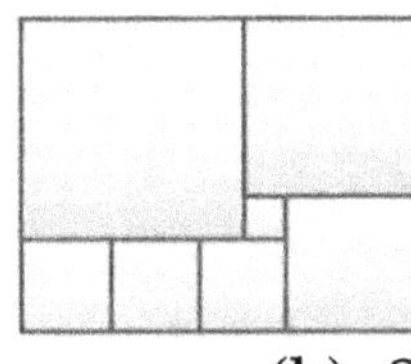

(a) 2   (b) 3

(c) 4   (d) 5

27. The shape of  looks like a _____

(a) cone   (b) cylinder

(c) sphere   (d) cube

Directions (28 & 29): There are three cats A, B and C. A is older than C and younger than B.

28. Who is the youngest?

(a) A   (b) B

(c) C   (d) None

29. Who is the oldest?

(a) A   (b) B

(c) C   (d) None

30. Which number should come in the middle?

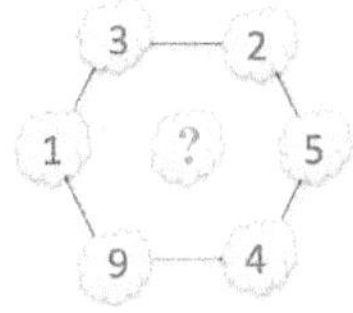

(a) 6   (b) 4

(c) 5   (d) 1

Name : __________

Max. Marks : 30

Number of Questions : 30

Time : 2 Hours

There is no negative marking in the test.

Directions (Qs. 1 to 3): In each of the questions given below, the series with one or more terms/letters/figures are missing marked with '?'. Choose the correct option to replace the '?' mark(s).

1.

(a)   (b)

(c)   (d)

2.

| 22 | ? | 44 | 55 | 66 |

(a)   33   (b)   23

(c)   67   (d)   77

3. 

(a)   19   (b)   13

(c)   16   (d)   15

4.   The weight of one toy clown is _ ○

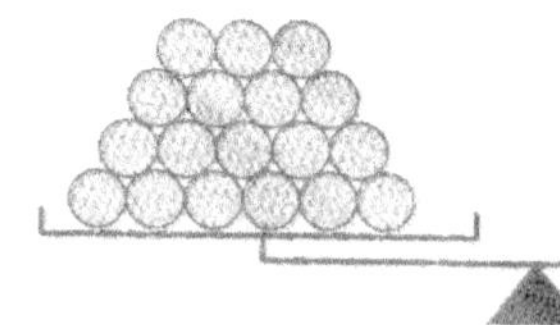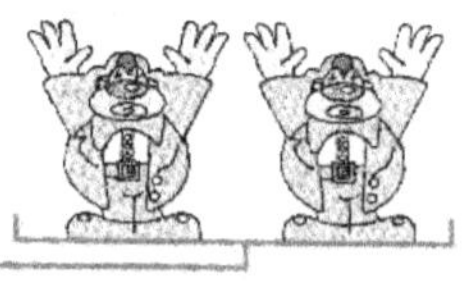

————— *Space for Rough Work* —————

(a) 10   (b) 18

(c) 12   (d) 9

5. Which ball is the heaviest?

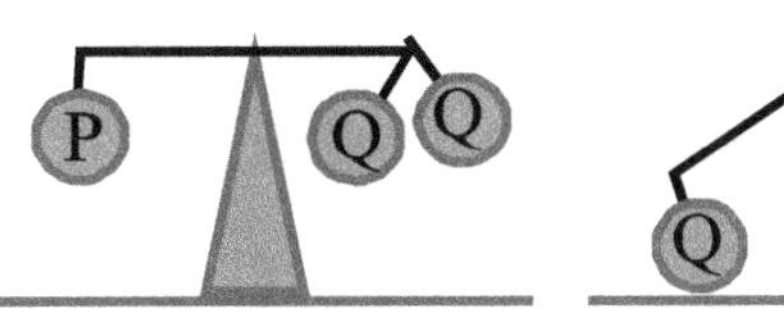

(a) Q

(b) R

(c) P

(d) Can't be determined

6. The microwave oven is _______  long and _______ tall.

(a) 3, 3   (b) 4, 3

(c) 5, 3   (d) 2, 3

7. There are _________ more circles than triangles in the adjoining picture.

(a) 13   (b) 11

(c) 14   (d) 15

Directions (Qs. 8 & 9): Find the odd one out.

8. (a)   (b)

    (c)   (d)

9. (a)   (b)

    (c)   (d)

Space for Rough Work

Directions (Qs. 10 & 11): Study the given picture and answer the following questions.

10. Number of apples on the tree is ___.

    (a) 4   (b) 6

    (c) 5   (d) 8

11. Number of apples under the tree is __________.

    (a) 4   (b) 3

    (c) 5   (d) 2

12. There are _________ flowers in each 4 equal groups of flowers.

    (a) 5   (b) 3

    (c) 2   (d) 4

13. The given figure() belong to group _________.

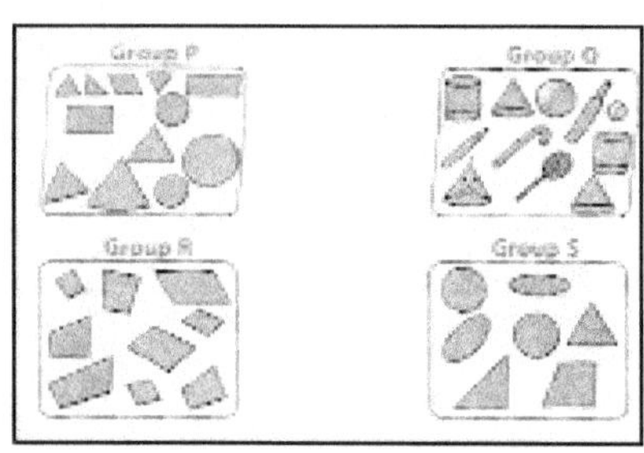

    (a) P   (b) Q

    (c) R   (d) S

Directions (Qs. 14 to 16) : There is a certain relationship between the pair of figure given on either side of : :. Identify the relationship of given pair and find the missing term.

14. 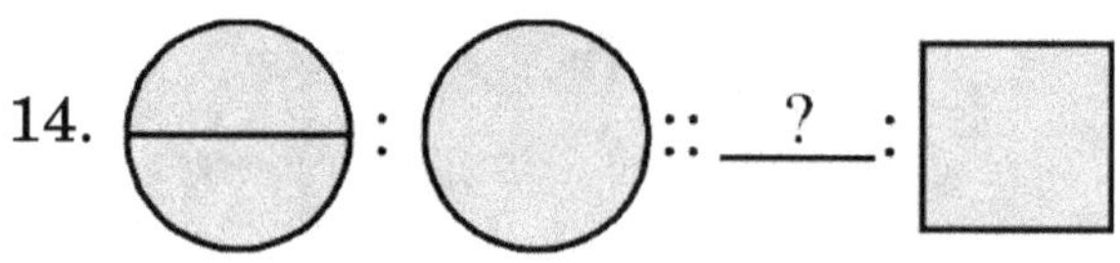

    (a)   (b)

    (c)   (d)

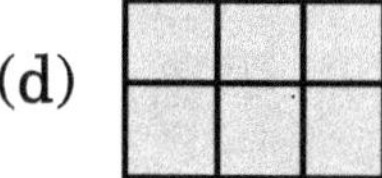

15. 

(a) 

(b) 

(c) 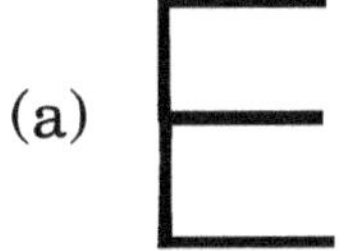

(d) 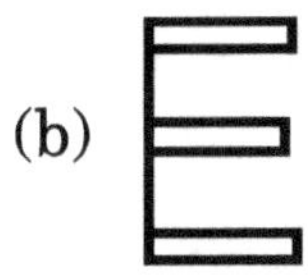

16. 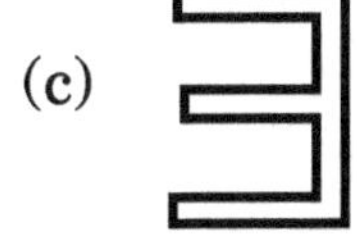

(a) 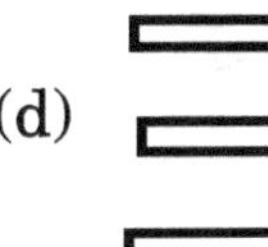

(b)

(c)

(d)

17. The position of the flower in the circle is __________.

(a) 3rd from the left end

(b) 4th from the left end

(c) 3rd from the right end

(d) In the centre

18. The penguin that is in the first position is __________.

(a) S

(b) T

(c) M

(d) J

19. Subtract the 3ʳᵈ number from the left of the 1ˢᵗ number and you will get the ______ number from the right end.

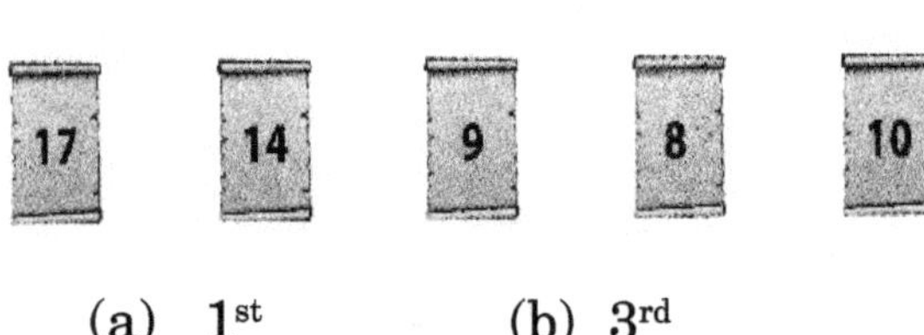

   (a) 1ˢᵗ   (b) 3ʳᵈ

   (c) 2ⁿᵈ   (d) 4ᵗʰ

Directions (Qs. 20 & 21): Look at the picture and answer the following questions.

20. There are ______ squares.

   (a) 4   (b) 2

   (c) 1   (d) 3

21. There are ______ circles.

   (a) 3   (b) 1

   (c) 5   (d) 2

22. Find the odd one out.

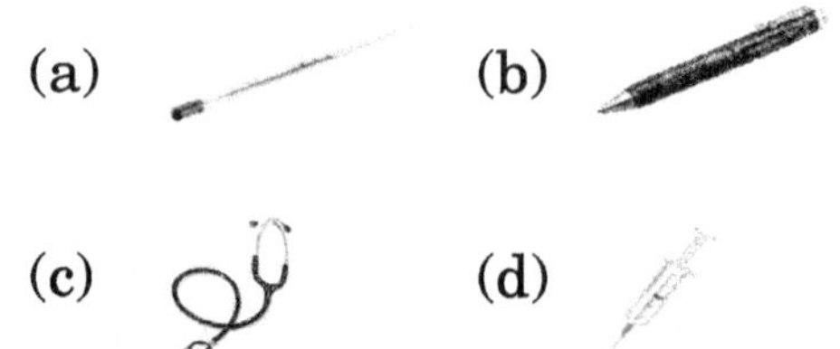

   (a)   (b)

   (c)   (d)

Directions (Qs. 23 & 24): Study the given picture and answer the following questions.

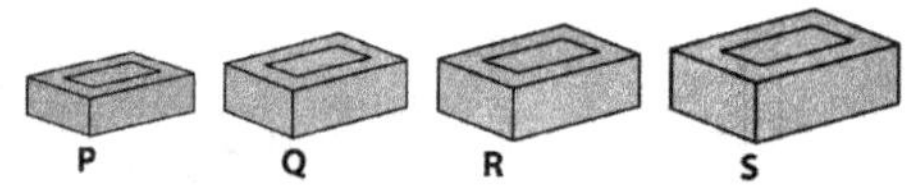

23. Which of the brick is thickest?

   (a) Q   (b) P

   (c) R   (d) S

24. Which of the brick is thinnest?

   (a) P   (b) S

   (c) Q   (d) R

Space for Rough Work

Directions (Qs. 25 & 26): Three children have different pets. These pets are dog, fish and a bird.

- Rohan's pet cannot fly.

- Ankur's pet does not bark.

- Pinki's pet lives in water.

25. Whose pet is dog?

   (a) Rohan   (b) Ankur

   (c) Pinki   (d) None

26. Which pet does Ankur has?

   (a) Bird   (b) Dog

   (c) Fish   (d) None

27. Which shape has the lowest number of sides?

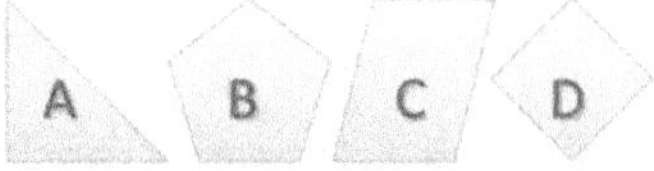

   (a) A   (b) B

   (c) C   (d) D

28. Shivam has 6 coins. He gave 4 away. How many coins is he left with?

   (a) 5   (b) 4

   (c) 3   (d) 2

29. How many cubes you should add to make a tower of 8 cubes ?

   (a) 1   (b) 2

   (c) 3   (d) 4

30. Look at the toy pyramid. Which ring is longest in size from the bottom ?

   (a) 3   (b) 6

   (c) 4   (d) 7

Space for Rough Work

Name : __________

Number of Questions : 30

Max. Marks : 30

Time : 2 Hours

There is no negative marking in the test.

1. Complete the figure pattern given below .

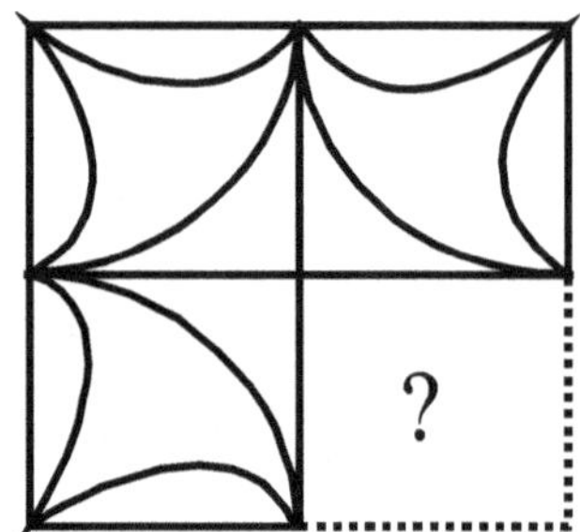

(a) 

(b)

(c) 

(d)

Directions (Qs. 2 & 3): In each of the questions given below, the series with one or more terms/letters/figures are missing marked with '?'. Choose the correct option to replace the '?' marks(s).

2. 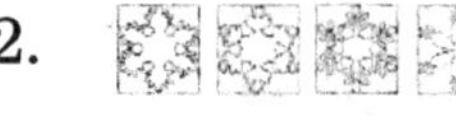

(a) 

(b) 

(c) 

(d) 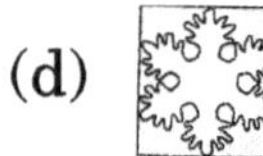

3. 

(a) 18, 15

(b) 12, 21

(c) 12, 15

(d) 12, 18

Space for Rough Work

4. Which is true about objects A, B and C?

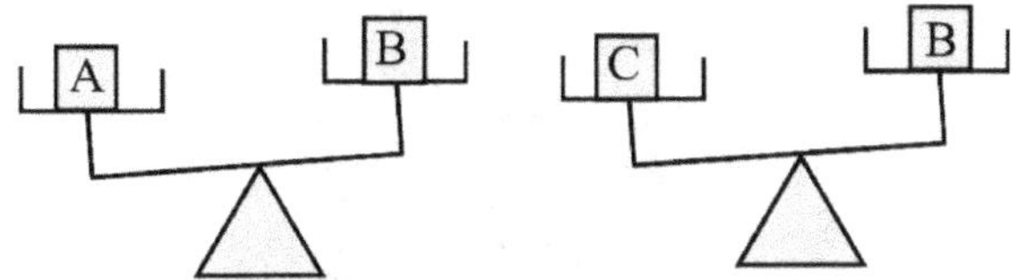

(a) A is lighter than B.

(b) A is as heavy as B.

(c) C is lighter than B.

(d) Both A and C are heavier than B.

5. If today is Sunday, then tomorrow will be __________.

(a) Wednesday (b) Monday

(c) Thursday   (d) Friday

6. Each ▭ stands for 1 unit. Stick P is ____ units longer than stick Q.

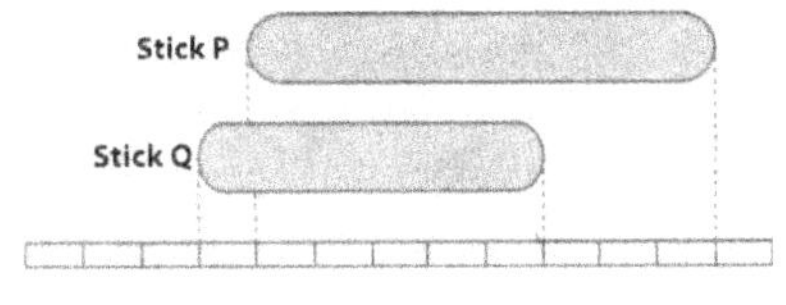

(a) 3   (b) 2

(c) 1   (d) 4

Directions (Qs. 7 & 8): Study the given figure and answer the following questions.

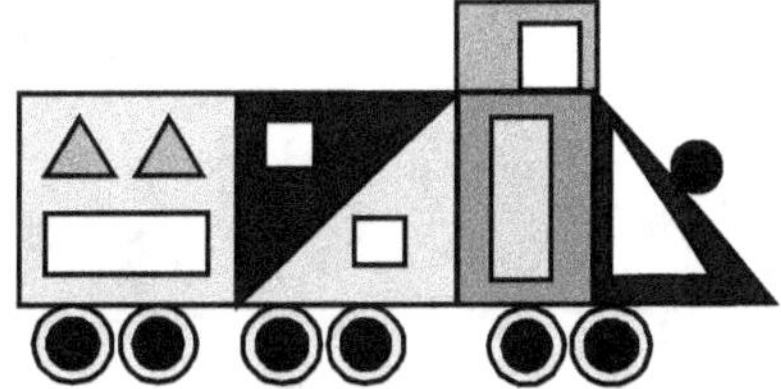

7. There are ______ circles and triangles altogether.

(a) 18   (b) 15

(c) 13   (d) 19

Space for Rough Work

8. There are _______ squares.

   (a) 4   (b) 5

   (c) 3   (d) 6

Directions (Qs. 9 & 10): Find the odd one out.

9. (a) 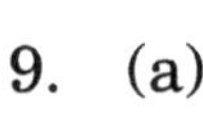   (b) 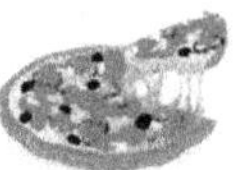

   (c)    (d) 

10. (a)    (b) 

    (c)    (d) 

Directions (Qs. 11 & 12): Observe the picture carefully and answer the following questions.

11. Number of students outside the school bus is _____.

    (a) 3   (b) 4

    (c) 5   (d) 2

12. Number of person inside the school bus is _____.

    (a) 1   (b) 2

    (c) 3   (d) 4

Space for Rough Work

13. How many planes are flying above the clouds?

(a) 3 (b) 2

(c) 4 (d) 5

14. There are ______ groups of 7 cherries.

(a) 4 (b) 4

(c) 2 (d) 6

Directions (Qs. 15 & 16): There is a certain relationship between the pair of figures given on either side of : :. Identify the relationship of given pair and find the missing term.

15. 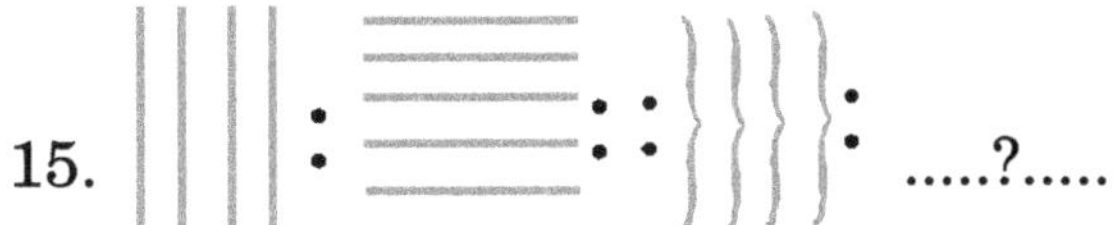 .....?.....

(a)  (b)

(c)  (d)

16.  .....?.....

(a) 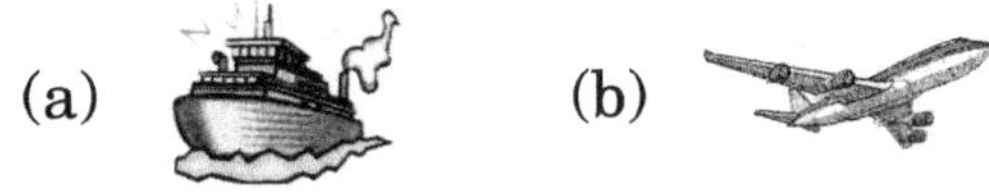 (b)

(c) 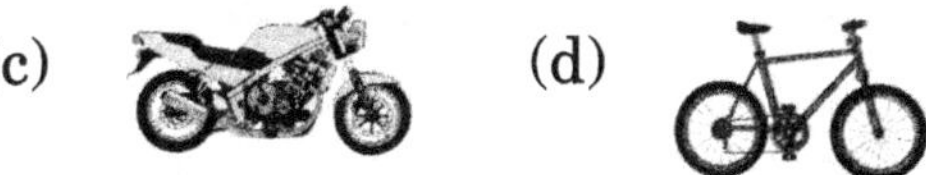 (d)

17. The 5th letter from the left end is _________.

A	D	C	B	E	G	I	O	K	P

(a) B   (b) E

(c) O   (d) G

18. The 8th number from the right end is _________.

1	5	6	9	13	14	20	12	7	3

(a) 6   (b) 13

(c) 9   (d) 12

Directions (19 & 20): Three children have different birth months, but were all born in the same year. Mayank was born in April. Anshul was born after Mayank but before Shubam.

19. Who is the youngest?

(a) Mayank   (b) Anshul

(c) Shubam   (d) None

20. Who is the oldest ?

(a) Anshul   (b) Mayank

(c) Shubam   (d) None

21. Neeraj has 4 apples. Sunny has one less apple than Neeraj. How many apples does Sunny has?

(a) 1   (b) 2

(c) 3   (d) 4

22. How many windows are there on the upper floor?

(a) 3   (b) 5

(c) 7   (d) 8

Space for Rough Work

23. How many stars are there inside the circle?

(a) 2   (b) 7

(c) 5   (d) 9

24. What is the missing number on the number line?

(a) 9   (b) 10

(c) 11   (d) 12

25. How many straight lines are there in the given picture?

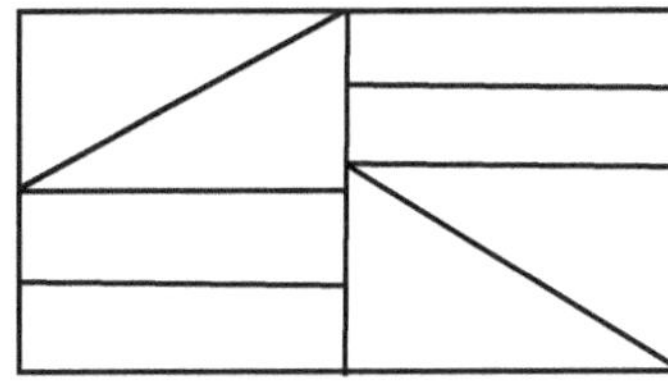

(a) 11   (b) 8

(c) 9   (d) 15

26. There are ____ triangles in the figure.

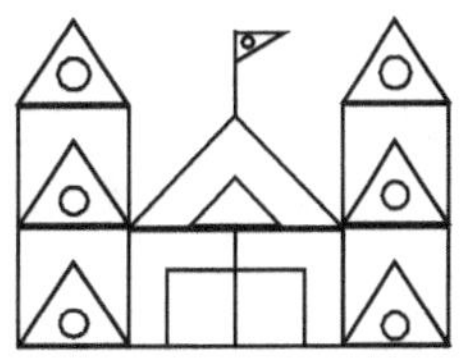

(a) 7   (b) 9

(c) 5   (d) 2

27. Find the odd one out.

(a) 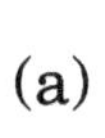   (b) 

(c)    (d) 

28. There is certain relationship between the pair of figure given on either side of : :. Identify the relationship of given and find the missing term.

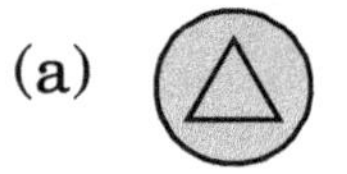 : 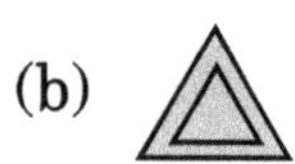 : :  : 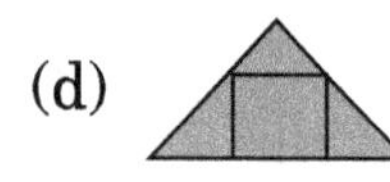

(a) 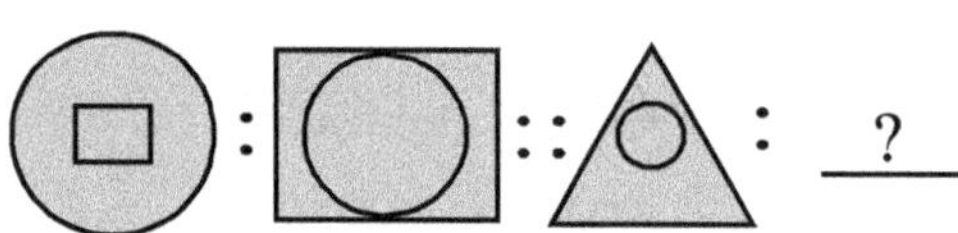

29. The brush is _____ units shorter than the pencil. (1 ▢ = 1 units)

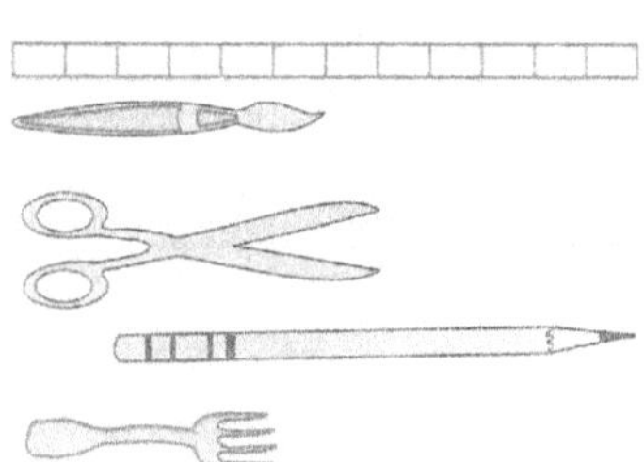

(a) 5   (b) 3

(c) 4   (d) 2

30. Find the missing numbers.

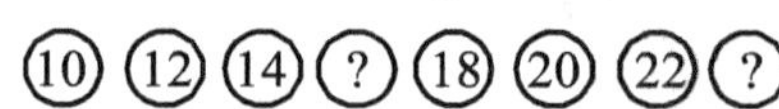

(a) 20, 24   (b) 18, 20

(c) 16, 24   (d) 20, 22

CYBER
MOCK TEST 1-3

OLYMPIAD
Mock Test 1

Name : ___________

Number of Questions : 25

Max. Marks : 25

Time : 2 Hours

There is no negative marking in the test.

1. Which of the following is NOT a type of computer?

   (a) Palmtop   (b) Laptop

   (c) Desktop   (d) Tabtop

2. Which of the following tasks a computer can do for you?

   (a) Play music   (b) Eat food

   (c) Drink water   (d) All of these.

3. Select the correct match.

   (i)    1. Palmtop

   (ii) 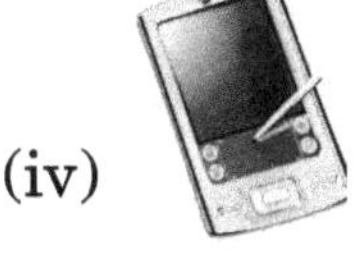   2. Laptop

   (iii)    3. Desktop Computer

   (iv)   4. Tablet

   (a) i-4, ii-3, iii-2, iv-1.

   (b) i-3, ii-4, iii-2, iv-1

   (c) i-1, ii-3, iii-2, iv-4

   (d) i-3, ii-4, iii-1, iv-2

Space for Rough Work

4. Which of the following part of a computer is used to take hard copy (copies information from the computer screen on a sheet of paper) from it?

(a) 

(b) 

(c) 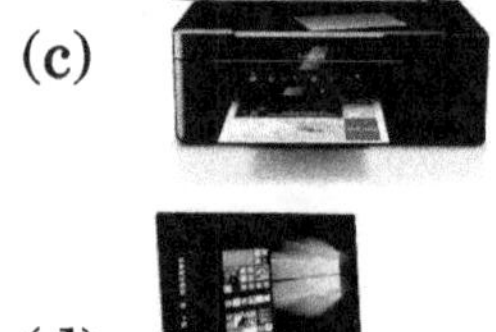

(d)

5. Which of the following is not a part of computer?

(a) 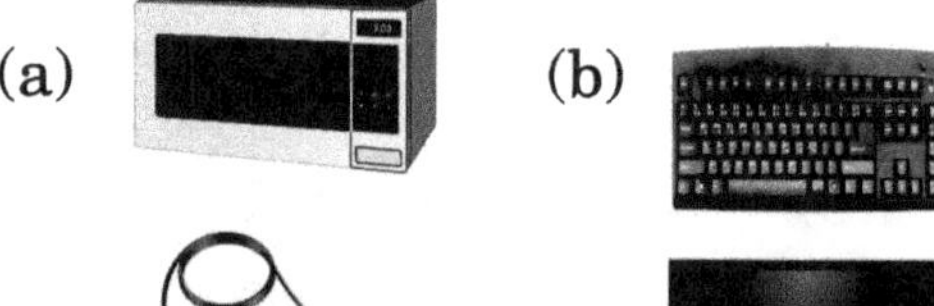   (b)

(c)    (d) 

6. Which of the following parts of a computer is used to point and select items on computer screen?

(a) 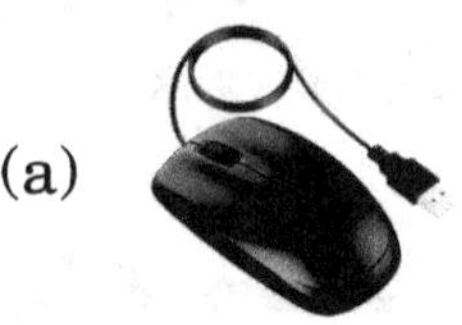

(b) 

(c) 

(d) 

7. Using a computer, we can

    (a) do weather forecasting

    (b) Search for information

    (c) Both (a) and (b)

    (d) None of the above

8. A smartphone can be used for ________.

   (a) playing games
   (b) listening music
   (c) video calling
   (d) all of these

9. Which of the following types of computers can be used while travelling ?

   (1)   (2)   (3)

   (a) Only 1   (b) Only 2
   (c) Both 2 & 3   (d) Both 1 & 3

10. Whatever is typed on keyboard, it can be seen on

   (a) Monitor   (b) Printer
   (c) Speaker   (d) CPU

11. Which of the following keys when pressed once, capitalizes each letter typed?

   (a) Shift   (b) Ctrl
   (c) CapsLock   (d) Tab

12. Which key is used to give space after words, alphabets or numbers? If pressed once, it gives the space of one character.

   (a) Space bar   (b) Enter
   (c) Shift   (d) Backspace

13. Pressing and releasing the mouse button means __________.

   (a) typing   (b) clicking
   (c) hitting   (d) pushing

14. If you want to do the following task,

   1. Selecting items
   2. Drawing pictures
   3. Opening a file.

   which of the following devices can you use?

   (a)    (b) 

   (c) 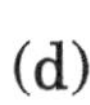   (d) 

15. A mouse has a wheel in the center which is called a ___________ ball.

    (a) touch   (b) scroll

    (c) track   (d) roller

16. What is the first step to start a computer?

    (a) Press the power button on UPS.

    (b) Switch on the monitor.

    (c) Press the power button on CPU.

    (d) Switch on the main power button.

17. Which of the following steps start a computer after main power is switched on?

    (a) Press the power button on UPS.

    (b) Switch on the monitor.

    (c) Press the power button on CPU.

    (d) All of these

18. To start a laptop, you just need to press ___________.

    (a) the window key

    (b) the power button available on the laptop

    (c) the enter key

    (d) the space bar key

19. Which of the following tools is used to draw the given shape?

    (a)   (b)

    (c)   (d)

20. Which of the following tools is not used to draw shapes?

    (a)   (b)

    (c)   (d)

———————————— *Space for Rough Work* ————————————

21. What is the use of the given tool?

    (a) It is used to erase your drawing.

    (b) It is used to fill the shapes with colour.

    (c) It is used to draw shapes.

    (d) None of these

22. Which of the following technologies allows you to interact with the smartphone or laptop with your fingers?

    (a) Interscreen

    (b) Pickscreen

    (c) Touchscreen

    (d) Dualscreen

23. What is an App?

    (a) Application software

    (b) Applicant

    (c) Accessibility

    (d) Applicator program

24. Which of the following is a gaming device?

    (a)    (b) 

    (c)    (d) 

25. Which of the following is a wearable computer?

    (a) Smart watch 

    (b) Google-glasses 

    (c) Smart-Ring 

    (d) All of these

OLYMPIAD Mock Test 2

Name : _______________

Number of Questions : 25

Max. Marks : 25

Time : 2 Hours

There is no negative marking in the test.

1. Select the correct statement about a computer.

   (a) It cannot solve arithmetic calculation.

   (b) It is a man-made machine and it is very fast.

   (c) You cannot play game on it.

   (d) It is not an electronic machine.

2. Which of the following is/are a man-made and electronic machine?

   (a)    (b) 

   (c)    (d) All of these

3. If you want to do the following task,

   (i) Listening music

   (ii) Watching movies

   (iii) Paying game

   (iv) Solve the mathematical operations

   Which of the following devices can you use?

   (a)    (b) 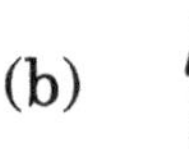

   (c)    (d) 

———————— Space for Rough Work ————————

4. Which of the following parts of a computer is used to control the overall working of a computer ?

(a) 

(b) 

(c) 

(d) 

5. Identify the picture for the given jumbled word.

    BOKEYARD

(a) 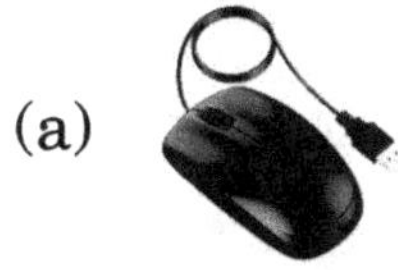   (b) 

(c)  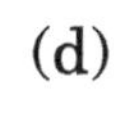   (d) 

6. Whatever you type on keyboard is shown on

(a) 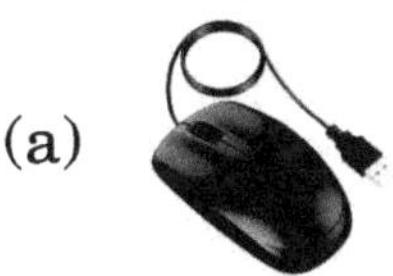   (b) 

(c)    (d) 

7. We type ________ on computer by the help of keyboard.

    (a) special symbols

    (b) digits

    (c) letters

    (d) all of these

8. Which of the following can be prepared using a computer in schools?

    (a) Students record

    (b) Time-table

    (c) Circulars

    (d) All of these

9. In school, computers are used to

   (a) Store the information about students

   (b) To sell the tickets

   (c) To monitor the trains timings

   (d) All of these

10. Which of the following is not an alphabet key?

   (a) L   (b))0

   (c) N   (d) O

11. To write something on a computer screen, we need a _______.

   (a) keyboard

   (b) scrolls

   (c) pen or pencil

   (d) both (a) & (b)

12. Which is the longest key on the keyboard?

   (a) Enter   (b) Shift

   (c) Space bar   (d) Backspace

13. Which of the following statement is correct for wireless mouse?

   (a) It does not require a click.

   (b) It does not need to be touched for operating.

   (c) It does not need cable.

   (d) It connects the computer with a cable.

14. Match the following:

	Column-1		Column-2
(i)	Scrolling	(1)	pressing and holding the mouse button and moving.
(ii)	Double-clicking	(2)	moving the mouse wheel up or down.
(iii)	Pointer	(3)	pressing the mouse button twice.
(iv)	Clicking and dragging	(4)	it is a symbol or graphical image on the computer monitor

   (a) i-2, ii-3, iii-4, iv-1

   (b) i-3, ii-4, iii-1, iv-2

   (c) i-4, ii-3, iii-1, iv-2

   (d) i-1, ii-3, iii-4, iv-2

Space for Rough Work

15. Which of the following statements is/are correct for a computer mouse?

    (a) It is controlled with hand and helps to draw.

    (b) It sits outside of the computer case.

    (c) It comes in many shapes and size.

    (d) All of these

16. Once the computer is on, a screen is displayed, which is called______.

    (a) desktop   (b) wallpaper

    (c) window   (d) picture

17. Which of the following parts of a computer helps us to select the shut down option in start menu?

    (a) 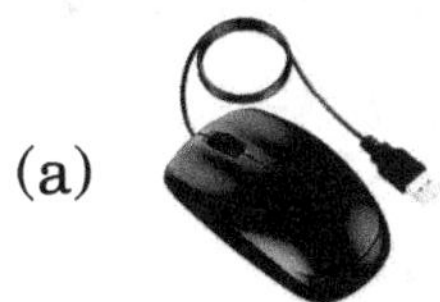   (b) 

    (c)    (d) Both (a) and (b)

18. Which of the following parts is used to keep the computer on, when there is a power failure?

    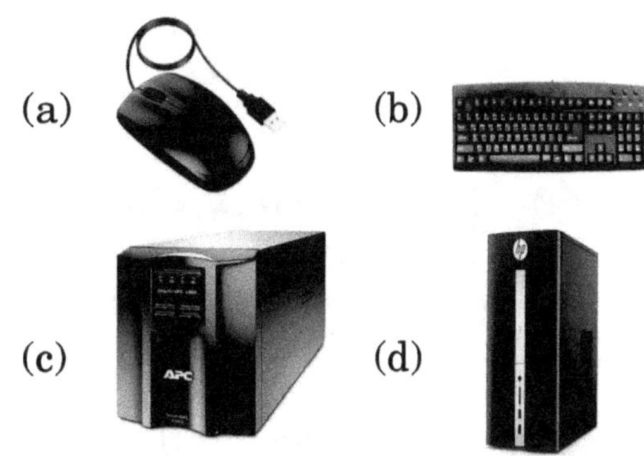

    (a)   (b)

    (c)   (d)

19. Which of the following tools helps you to draw the free-form lines shown below?

    (a) ∿   (b) ◯

    (c) \   (d) Both (a) & (c)

Space for Rough Work

20. The given set of tools and shapes is found in________.

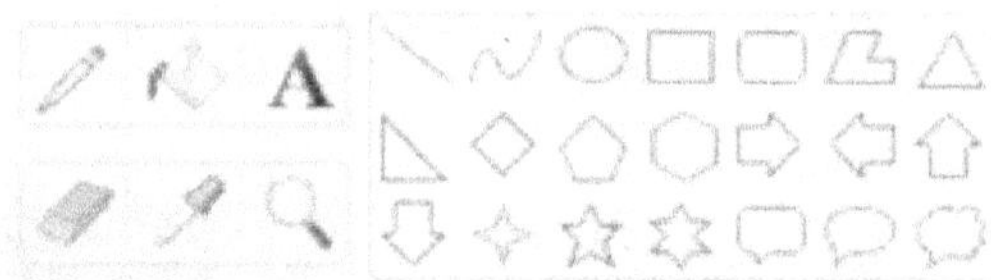

(a) Ribbon area
(b) Drawing area
(c) Workspace area
(d) none of these

21. Which of the following tools is used to completely fill the colour in the closed shapes?

(a)    (b) 

(c)    (d) None of these

22. In which of the following devices can you run apps?

(a) 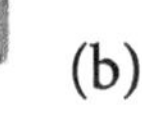   (b) 

(c)    (d) 

23. Which of the following devices comes with touch-screen?

(a) 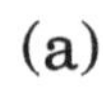   (b) 

(c)    (d) All of these.

24. Which of the following tasks can be done by a smartwatch?
(a) Playing games
(b) Solving Sums
(c) Listening music
(d) All of these

25. Identify the given device.
1. It is a watch that you can wear on your wrist.
2. It can perform all the tasks done by a smart-phone.

(a) smartwrist   (b) world clock
(c) hand   (d) smartwatch

Name : _______________

Max. Marks : 25

Number of Questions : 25

Time : 2 Hours

There is no negative marking in the test.

1. Computer is also known as a smart machine because

    (a) it works very fast and never gets tired.

    (b) it does not make mistake on its own

    (c) it can solve complex problems very easily.

    (d) all of these

2. Which of the following is/are correct about a computer?

    (a) It is an error prone machine

    (b) It does have emotions

    (c) It does have knowledge (IQ)

    (d) None of these

3. CPU is called the brain of the computer. What does CPU stands for?

    (a) Control Processing Unit

    (b) Calculations Processing Unit

    (c) Central Processing Unit

    (d) None of these

4. Select the odd one out. (regarding parts of a computer)

    (a) 

    (b) 

    (c) 

    (d) 

———————————— Space for Rough Work ————————————

5. Match the following.

Column-1 Column-2

(i)    (1) It is used to type letters into the computer

(ii)    (2) It is known as brain of a computer.

(iii)    (3) It is used to take a computer copies of information from the computer screen on a sheet of paper.

(iv)    (4) It is used to watch movies.

(a) i-4, ii-1, iii-2, iv-3

(b) i-2, ii-3, iii-4, iv-1

(c) i-3, ii-4, iii-2, iv-1

(d) i-1, ii-3, iii-4, iv-2

6. Identify the parts of computer marked as 1 and 2 and select the correct statements.

1.

2.

(a) 1. It is known as the brain of a computer.

    2. It is used to take of copies of information from the computer screen on a sheet of paper.

(b) 1. It is used to type letters.

    2. It is used to point items on computer.

(c) 1. It is used to listen to sound.

    2. It is known as speaker.

(d) None of these

Space for Rough Work

7. To listen songs on your computer, you should use _______.

(a)   (b)

(c)   (d)

8. Which of the following statements is incorrect about the use of a computer?

(a) A computer can be used to solve arithmetical problems.

(b) We can play games on a computer.

(c) We can watch movies on a computer

(d) We use pencil and paper to draw pictures on a computer.

9. Which of the following games can be played on a computer?

(a) Car Racing   (b) Cricket

(c) Football   (d) All of these

10. Which of the following pictures do not show the use of computer?

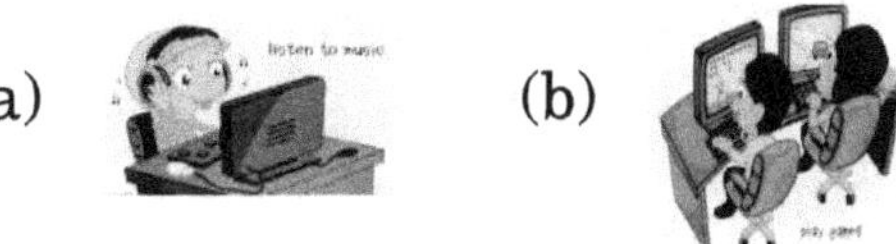

(a)   (b)

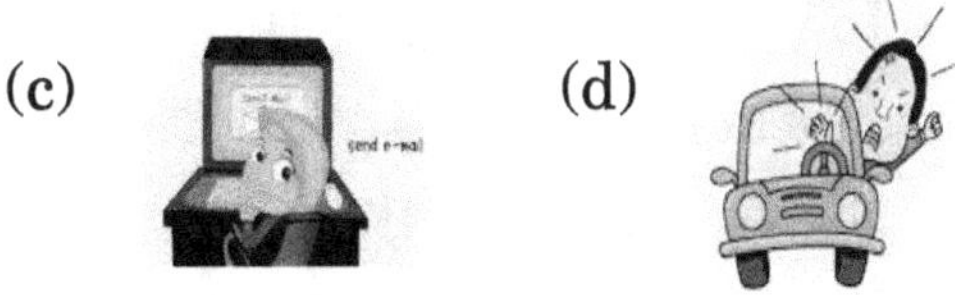

(c)   (d)

11. Which of the following statements is incorrect?

(a) Newspapers are printed with the help of computers.

(b) Computer is used to make mobile games.

(c) Computer is used for building layouts.

(d) Computer is used for making kitchen appliances.

Space for Rough Work
---

12. The keys from 0 to 9 are called
    ______________ keys.

    (a) special   (b) numeric

    (c) alphabet   (d) function

13. Which of the following keys would
    be used to type your date of birth
    and name?

    (a) Numeric key

    (b) Alphabet key

    (c) Special key

    (d) All of these

14. Identify the keyboard key function
    marked as 1 and 2 and select the
    correct statements:

    1.    2. 

    (a) 1. Delete key is used to
             erase character to the left
             of the cursor.

         2. Backspace key is used to
             erase character to right
             of the cursor.

    (b) 1. Delete key is used to
             erase character.

    2. Backspace key is used to
        give a small gap between
        two characters.

    (c) 1. Delete key is used to
             erase character to the
             right of cursor.

         2. Backspace used to erase
             character to left of the
             cursor.

    (d) None of these

15. Which of the following mouse
    actions displays a list of commands
    on screen?

    (a) Right click

    (b) Drag and drop

    (c) Scrolling

    (d) Left click

16. Which of the following functions is
    used for opening a file on computer
    by mouse?

    (a) Single left click

    (b) Double left click

    (c) Single right click

    (d) Double right click

17. A mouse has________ buttons.

    (a) 3   (b) 2

    (c) 4   (d) 5

18. Which of the following options safely shutsdown the computer and then starts it again?

    (a) Shutdown   (b) Hibernate

    (c) Logoff   (d) Restart

19. When a computer starts, the sequence of actions done by the computer to get everything ready for use is called

    (a) logging   (b) booting

    (c) clicking   (d) tapping

20. Which of the following steps should we follow after shutting down the computer?

    (a) Switch off the UPS power button.

    (b) Switch off the main power button.

    (c) Switch off the CPU.

    (d) First (a) & then (b)

21. The figure given below is used to......

    Colors

    (a) choose the tools and shapes for your drawing.

    (b) fill up the picture with different colour.

    (c) choose the color for your drawing.

    (d) both (b) & (c)

22. Which of the following tools is/are used when you do the given tasks while drawing?

    (1) To draw a circle shape.

    (2) To draw the rectangle inside the circle.

    (3) To fill the shape with colour.

    (a)   (b)

    (c)   (d) All of these

Space for Rough Work

23. Select the correct match.

(i) ⭘   (1) It is used for erasing, if you make a mistake.

(ii)   (2) It is used to draw circles.

(iii) ☐   (3) It is used to fill the shape with colour.

(iv)   (4) It is used to draw rectangle.

(a) i-2, ii-3, iii-4, iv-1

(b) i-3, ii-2, iii-1, iv-4

(c) i-4, ii-3, iii-2, iv-1

(d) i-2, ii-1, iii-4, iv-3

24. The tool used to draw straight lines of different thickness, colour and length in MS-Paint is ______.

(a)   (b) ⭘

(c)   (d) △

25. Identify the following.

1. It can fit in your pocket and are small in size.

2. You can carry it wherever you go.

3. It has a touch-screen.

(a) Laptops

(b) Smart-phone

(c) Desktop computer

(d) All of these

Space for Rough Work

HINTS & EXPLANATIONS

ENGLISH

MOCK TEST 1

ANSWER KEY

1	(d)	8	(a)	15	(b)	22	(c)	29	(b)
2	(c)	9	(b)	16	(b)	23	(b)	30	(a)
3	(d)	10	(a)	17	(c)	24	(c)	31	(b)
4	(a)	11	(b)	18	(c)	25	(c)	32	(a)
5	(b)	12	(a)	19	(a)	26	(a)	33	(b)
6	(c)	13	(b)	20	(b)	27	(d)	34	(b)
7	(b)	14	(d)	21	(c)	28	(b)	35	(b)

1. **(d)** Cow; rest are water animals while cow is a land animal.

2. **(c)** Cat; rest are parts of computer, whereas cat is an animal.

3. **(d)** Pencil; rest are used in the kitchen.

4. **(a)** Shirt

5. **(b)** Washing Machine

6. **(c)** Umbrella

7. **(b)** Banana

8. **(a)** Spoon

9. **(b)** Salt

10. **(a)** Potato

11. **(b)** Gentlemen

12. **(a)** Lioness

13. **(b)** Fawn

14. **(d)** Tadpole

15. **(b)** He goes there everyday.

16. **(b)** The wolves were howling.

17. **(c)** I have two pencil boxes.

18. **(c)** The sheep are in the ground.

19. **(a)** Awake

20. **(b)** Easy

21. **(c)** Smooth

22. **(c)** My name is Riya. I'm a teacher.

23. **(b)** I teach children.

24. **(c)** I go to school.

25. **(c)** I write on the blackboard with a chalk.

26. **(a)** Ramu was a kind elephant.

27. **(d)** A rabbit came to Ramu for help.

28. **(b)** After seeing the lion, Ramu ran away.

29. **(b)** Thank you.

30. **(a)** I am 7 years old.

31. **(b)** No, he is my cousin.

32. **(a)** Yes, it's a lovely place.

33. **(b)** I am fine, how about you?

34. **(b)** Oh! Did you take any medicine?

35. **(b)** Student: Yes, Ma'am.

MOCK TEST 2

ANSWER KEY

1	(b)	8	(a)	15	(a)	22	(b)	29	(a)
2	(b)	9	(b)	16	(d)	23	(b)	30	(c)
3	(b)	10	(d)	17	(c)	24	(a)	31	(b)
4	(c)	11	(b)	18	(d)	25	(b)	32	(a)
5	(d)	12	(a)	19	(d)	26	(b)	33	(d)
6	(d)	13	(b)	20	(a)	27	(b)	34	(b)
7	(c)	14	(a)	21	(b)	28	(c)	35	(c)

1. **(b)** Glass
2. **(b)** Table
3. **(b)** Television
4. **(c)** Truck
5. **(d)** Lion. Rest are human beings
6. **(d)** Town. As the rest are directions, town is a territorial entity.
7. **(c)** Sun. As the rest are planets and Sun is a star.
8. **(a)** Bread and Butter
9. **(b)** Sun and Moon
10. **(d)** Give and Take
11. **(b)** You bite with your teeth.
12. **(a)** You write with a pen.
13. **(b)** You smell with your nose.
14. **(a)** Watch a movie
15. **(a)** Dare
16. **(d)** Torch
17. **(c)** Shall
18. **(d)** Sir
19. **(d)** The girl is playing with a kite.
20. **(a)** The girl wearing purple top is riding a bicycle.
21. **(b)** The boy wearing orange T-shirt is playing with football.
22. **(b)** The girl wearing blue top is skipping the rope.
23. **(b)** Rainbow
24. **(a)** The author found it to be wonderful.
25. **(b)** There are seven colours in the rainbow.
26. **(b)** One colour that is not there in a rainbow is black.
27. **(b)** To reach and touch the rainbow.
28. **(c)** Yes, may I know who is calling?
29. **(a)** Shopkeeper: May I help you? Customer: Yes, do you have double door fridges?
30. **(c)** Yes, I was looking for a room.
31. **(b)** Yes, but she has told me to come early.
32. **(a)** Yes, I really like them.
33. **(d)** I was sleeping.
34. **(b)** Doctor: How are you? Patient: Better, thanks!
35. **(c)** Ma'am! I was not well.

MOCK TEST 3

ANSWER KEY

1	(b)	9	(b)	17	(a)	25	(b)	33	(b)
2	(b)	10	(b)	18	(c)	26	(b)	34	(a)
3	(b)	11	(c)	19	(b)	27	(b)	35	(a)
4	(a)	12	(a)	20	(b)	28	(a)	36	(c)
5	(d)	13	(b)	21	(a)	29	(c)	37	(c)
6	(c)	14	(b)	22	(b)	30	(a)	38	(b)
7	(d)	15	(a)	23	(a)	31	(a)	39	(d)
8	(c)	16	(b)	24	(d)	32	(d)	40	(c)

1. **(b)** Top
2. **(b)** Flower
3. **(b)** Bicycle
4. **(a)** Boat
5. **(d)** Cabbage. Rest are fruits, cabbage is a vegetable.
6. **(c)** Chocolate. Rest are to be read; chocolate is something meant to be eaten.
7. **(d)** Classroom. Rest are human beings, classroom is a type of building.
8. **(c)** Cub. Rest are animal homes, cub is a lion's baby.
9. **(b)** Lion
10. **(b)** Father
11. **(c)** Knife
12. **(a)** Fridge
13. **(b)** A group of leopards is called leap.
14. **(b)** A kangaroo chortles.
15. **(a)** My Mom is the greatest mom.
16. **(b)** She is there for me whenever I need her.
17. **(a)** She cooks tasty food.
18. **(c)** She is never in a foul mood.
19. **(b)** My name is Lona. I am a lion.
20. **(b)** I stay in a den.
21. **(a)** My young one is called a cub.
22. **(b)** My group is called pride.
23. **(a)** This is a scene of a jungle.
24. **(d)** This picture does show not zebra.
25. **(b)** The animals are drinking water.
26. **(b)** The birds are flying.
27. **(b)** Shreya: Your house is so beautiful!
Manoj: Thanks.
28. **(a)** I'm so sorry.
29. **(c)** Harris: Can you click my photograph?
Nancy: Yes sure.

30 (a) Doctor: How are you now?
Patient: Much better.

31.(a) We are planning a party for mom.

32.(d) Sure, I will come.

33.(b) A group of owls is called a parliament.

34.(a) We must respect our elders.

35.(a) I have to reach early or I will be late.

36.(c) I wanted to go out and play but I could not go.

37.(c) Sun

38.(b) Zebra

39.(d) George Washington was the President of USA.

40.(c) Tomorrow is Tuesday.

MOCK TEST 4

ANSWER KEY									
1	(a)	9	(a)	17	(a)	25	(d)	33	(b)
2	(b)	10	(a)	18	(a)	26	(a)	34	(b)
3	(b)	11	(a)	19	(b)	27	(d)	35	(c)
4	(a)	12	(b)	20	(b)	28	(c)	36	(b)
5	(a)	13	(c)	21	(d)	29	(b)	37	(c)
6	(a)	14	(b)	22	(d)	30	(a)	38	(c)
7	(a)	15	(b)	23	(c)	31	(a)	39	(c)
8	(b)	16	(a)	24	(b)	32	(c)	40	(d)

1. (a) Brain

2. (b) Balloons

3. (b) Fireman

4. (a) Deer

5. (a) You play cricket with a bat.

6. (a) We must never make war but make peace.

7. (a) Soap and Water

8. (b) In and Out

9. (a) I, Seema and Dinesh went by car. We enjoyed a lot.

10.(a) Mr. Shaan is a teacher. He teaches in a school.

11.(a) Mother: Get ready, quickly! You are getting late.

12.(b) I saw an owl on the tree.

13.(c) The man is hiding behind the sofa.

14.(b) There is a wall behind the man.

15.(b) The two boys are fighting with each other.

16.(a) He

17.(a) His

18.(a) You

19.(b) He wanted to swim in the pool.

20.(b) When you are crying, you are sad.

21. (d) Table, chair and almirah are furniture while kitchen is a section of the house.

22. (d) Train, bus and car move on road; ship moves in sea.

23. (c) February is the month, others are days.

24. (b) Cabbage is the vegetable, others are fruits.

25. (d) Horse is a land animal while others live in water.

26. (a) A washerman

27. (d) In the night

28. (c) When donkey saw itself alone, it began to bray. A donkey brays.

29. (b) Yes, it's mine.

30. (a) No, he left early today.

31. (a) Yes, I am going there.

32. (c) You have a wonderful house.

33. (b) No, I am still doing it.

34. (b) Farhan : He is my friend.

35. (c) Oh, that's sad.

36. (b) Hair

37. (c) Ankle

38. (c) Mahatma Gandhi is the Father of the Nation.

39. (c) Jack and Jill went up the hill.

40. (d) 2nd October is Gandhi Jayanti.

MOCK TEST 5

ANSWER KEY

1	(c)	8	(a)	15	(d)	22	(b)	29	(a)
2	(c)	9	(b)	16	(a)	23	(b)	30	(b)
3	(b)	10	(a)	17	(c)	24	(c)	31	(d)
4	(c)	11	(c)	18	(b)	25	(d)	32	(d)
5	(a)	12	(d)	19	(b)	26	(c)	33	(a)
6	(b)	13	(b)	20	(b)	27	(a)	34	(a)
7	(a)	14	(c)	21	(a)	28	(b)	35	(c)

1. (c) Watermelon

2. (c) Plant

3. (b) Spinach

4. (c) Sunflower

5. (a) Eyes

6. (b) Together is the correct word.

7. (a) Crocodile is the correct word.

8. (a) Doctor is the correct word.

9. (b) I am a policeman.

10. (a) My work is to catch thieves.

11. (c) Dog. Dog is not a wild animal.

12. (d) Muskmelon; rest are all vegetables. Muskmelon is a fruit.

13. (b) Soldier; rest can be seen in a hospital. A soldier is a part of the army.

14.(c) Student; rest can be seen in a post office. A student is a part of a school.

15.(d) Deer; rest are a part of school. Deer is an animal.

16.(a) An invitation to a birthday.

17.(c) Harshit's

18.(b) In the evening. The time is 4:30 p.m. P.M. means after 12 noon.

19.(b) At home. We can make out that since the address of the house is given.

20.(b) U.M. Punj

21.(a) 'An apple a day, keeps the doctor away'.

22.(b) Healthy food consists of fruit and vegetables.

23.(b) Milk and curd make your bones and teeth strong.

24.(c) Healthy food keeps diseases away from us.

25.(d) Ved: Great! Have fun.

26.(c) Sneha: I want to, but I have some work at home.

27.(a) Sumit: I don't want to play football.

28.(b) Son: Sure, dad.

29.(a) New Delhi is the capital of India.

30.(b) What did he say?

31.(d) His sister stays in Paris.

32.(d) I like milk but it should be cold.

33.(a) I couldn't come because I was not well.

34.(a) A nightingale sings.

35.(c) Shreya did not eat anything today. Now she's feeling hungry.

MATHEMATICS

MOCK TEST 1

ANSWER KEY									
1	(c)	9	(a)	17	(b)	25	(a)	33	(d)
2	(a)	10	(c)	18	(a)	26	(b)	34	(b)
3	(b)	11	(c)	19	(b)	27	(c)	35	(c)
4	(d)	12	(a)	20	(c)	28	(d)	36	(b)
5	(c)	13	(b)	21	(b)	29	(a)	37	(c)
6	(d)	14	(d)	22	(b)	30	(c)	38	(d)
7	(c)	15	(d)	23	(b)	31	(b)	39	(c)
8	(c)	16	(c)	24	(c)	32	(c)	40	(d)

1. (c) An arrow is made of 7 straight lines.

2. (a) A football has curved face, so it rolls.

3. (b) Book, brick and eraser have shape like cuboid.

4. (d) There are 7 monkeys in the picture.

5. (c) There are nine ducks in the given picture. If we remove 4 ducks, then 5 ducks are left in the picture.

$9 - 4 = 5$

6. (d) There are 7 mangoes in the given option (d) and the counting given in the circle is 6. So, this is the wrong combination.

7. (c) Balls given, $2 + 1 + 3 = 6$

8. (c) $16 < 23 < 31 < 32$

9. (a) Smileys drawn by Tiya = 2

Total smileys = 5

Smileys drawn by Tarun

$= 5 - 2 = 3$

10. (c) Gungun has $7 + 1 = 8$ candies.

11. (c)

Cars left = $7 - 2 = 5$

12. (a) Number of people sitting in taxi = 7

People get down = 3

Number of people continued the journey = $7 - 3 = 4$

13. (b) $A \rightarrow 9 - 9 = 0$

$B \rightarrow 8 - 1 = 7$

$C \rightarrow 7 - 6 = 1$

$D \rightarrow 4 + 2 = 6$

14. (d) Hen lays eggs = 7

Eggs taken away by man = 7 (all the eggs)

Eggs left = 7 − 7 = 0

= Zero

15. (d) Rimjhim has 4 dolls + 2 teddy bears + 1 toy car = 7 toys

16. (c) There are 5 numbers 1, 6, 9, 8, 2 which are less than 10.

17. (b) Here, A = 5 + 1 = 6

B = 10 + 1 = 11

18. (a) Friends have come = 6

Friends yet to come = 7

Total friends = 6 + 7 = 13

19. (b) Total number of children in the bus = 5 + 6 + 2 = 13

20. (c)

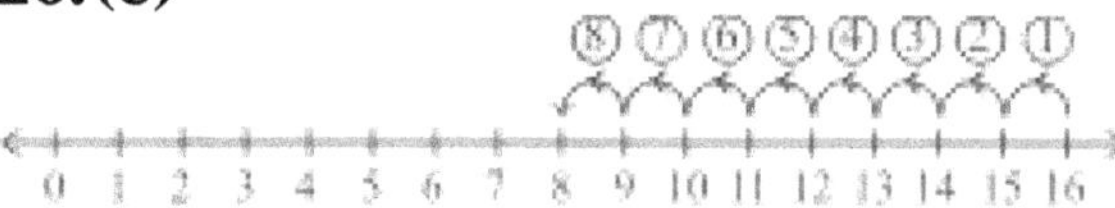

Jay ends up on 8 after counting 8 steps backwards.

21. (b)

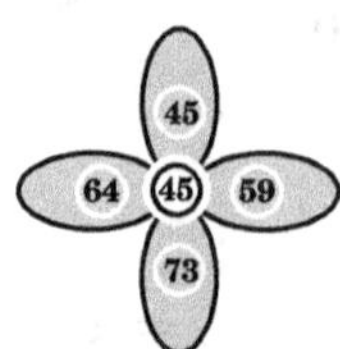

40 has 0 ones and it lies between 37 and 43.

22. (b) 45 is the smallest number so, honeybee writes 45 at the centre of the flower.

23. (b) Banana (24) < Mango (32) < Guava (40) < Orange (45)

Chintu buys bananas the least.

24. (c) Rupal has pencils = 19

Riya has pencils = 14

Now, 19 − 14 = 5

So, Rupal has 5 pencils more than Riya.

25. (a) Total pencils = 25

Group of 10 pencils = 2

Pencils used = 20

Pencils will left = 25 − 20 = 5

26. (b) Bucket holds more water than glass, mug and jug.

27. (c) ₹20 + ₹10 + ₹50 + ₹5 = ₹85

28. (d) The value of fruit basket = ₹50 + ₹5 + ₹2 = ₹57

29. (a) The length of the pencil is about 7 paper clips.

30. (c) There are 4 fishes that have stripes.

31. (b) 9 fishes are swimming in left direction.

32. (c) Total number of fishes = 15

33. (d) ⇨ is required to complete the pattern.

34. (b) Given pattern and pattern given in option (b) are similar.

1 2 1 2 1 2 1 2 1 2

35. (c) Tenth month of the year is October. The month comes after October is November. So, Ronald was born in November.

36. (b) 1 ten and 4 ones = 14

37. (c) Strawberry is the lightest object out of the given objects.

38. (d) Clock (d) is showing 7 o'clock.

39. (c) Square is not a solid shape.

40. (d) The given dot pattern has 3 tens and 3 ones. So, the number obtain is 30 + 3 = 33 = Thirty-three.

MOCK TEST 2

ANSWER KEY

1	(d)	9	(c)	17	(a)	25	(d)	33	(b)
2	(c)	10	(d)	18	(d)	26	(d)	34	(d)
3	(a)	11	(c)	19	(d)	27	(b)	35	(c)
4	(b)	12	(c)	20	(b)	28	(a)	36	(d)
5	(b)	13	(b)	21	(b)	29	(d)	37	(c)
6	(b)	14	(d)	22	(c)	30	(b)	38	(b)
7	(c)	15	(c)	23	(c)	31	(c)	39	(c)
8	(b)	16	(b)	24	(a)	32	(a)	40	(b)

1. (d) 3 comes between 2 and 4.

2. (c)

5 flowers + 3 flowers = 8 flowers

3. (a) Number of birds on the branch = 8

Birds flew away = 4

Number of birds left = 8 − 4 = 4

4. (b) There are 10 circles in the given picture.

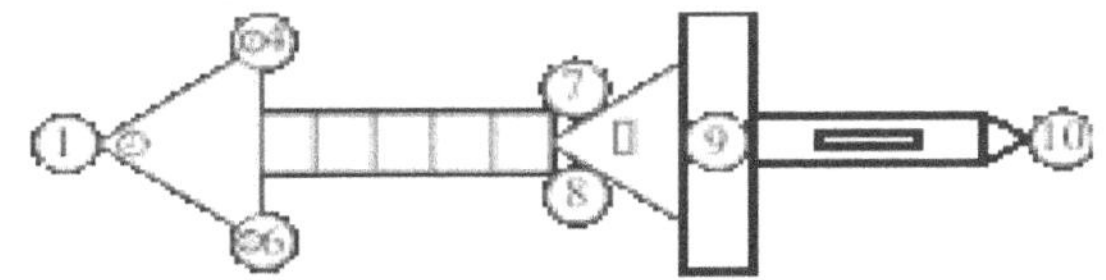

5. (b) The mat is 6 paces long.

6. (b) Bucket can contain more glasses of water because vessel that is larger in size contains more liquid.

7. (c) The distance between the two trees is 7 sticks.

8. (b) He collected money = ₹ 10 + ₹ 5 + ₹ 2 + ₹ 1 + ₹ 20 = ₹ 38

9. (c) Cost of one chocolate = ₹ 5

Cost of four chocolates = ₹ 5 + ₹ 5 + ₹ 5 + ₹ 5 = ₹ 20

10. (d) Hour hand is at 9

Minute hand is on 12

Thus, time is 9:00.

11. (c) Pattern given and pattern (c) are similar.

12. (c) Hand bag is the heaviest.

13. (b) Thursday comes after Wednesday and before Friday.

14. (d) For 8:00, hour hand points towards 8 and minute hand points towards 12. So, option (d) is correct.

15. (c) 16 − 4 = 12

16. (b) Total ice-creams = 78

Ice-cream melted = 25

Ice-cream left = 78 - 25 = 53

17. (a) Apples sold on Monday = 38

Apples sold on Tuesday = 41

Apples sold altogether = 38 + 41 = 79

18.(d) Dice is a solid shape.

19.(d) $50 > 47 > 34 > 11$

20.(b) Aisha has leaves = 3

She needs = 8

Akram gives her = $8 - 3 = 5$

21.(b)

$7 - 2 = 5$ bottles.

22.(c)

Aditi lost = $6 - 4 = 2$

23.(c) Tiya's age = 7 years

Her brother's age = $7 + 5$

$= 12$ years

24.(a) Total butterflies were there in the beginning = $6 + 3 = 9$

25.(d) 7 tens and 6 ones = 76

26.(d) The abacus is representing 5 tens and 1 ones. So, the number is 51.

The number name is fifty-one.

27.(b) Basket-1 = 10 mangoes

Basket-2 = 6 mangoes

Basket-3 = 3 mangoes

Total mangoes = $10 + 6 + 3 = 19$

28.(a) Abacus is representing 3 tens and 6 ones.

29.(d) Ball rolls on the surface.

30.(b) Total money collected by Saurabh and his friends

$= ₹\ 50 + ₹\ 10 + ₹\ 20 + ₹\ 5 + ₹\ 2 + ₹\ 1 = ₹\ 88$

31.(c) There are 5 mangoes in the basket.

32.(a) Mango = 5

Banana = 4

Apple = 6

Watermelon = 2

Apple is maximum in number in the basket.

33.(b) Total number of fruits

$= 5 + 4 + 6 + 2 = 17$

34.(d) The month between September and November is October.

35.(c) Rahul has shirts = 35

His brother has shirts = 12

Total shirts = $35 + 12 = 47$

36.(d) Train is heaviest.

37.(c) Passengers in the bus = 54

Passengers get off = 23

Passengers left = $54 - 23 = 31$

31 passengers are left in the bus.

38.(b) 18

39.(c) 3 as $8 - 3 = 5$

40.(b)

Tens	Ones
1	0
+	5
1	5

Now, 15 children are playing in the park.

MOCK TEST 3

ANSWER KEY

1	(c)	8	(c)	15	(d)	22	(b)	29	(c)
2	(b)	9	(b)	16	(c)	23	(b)	30	(b)
3	(b)	10	(c)	17	(b)	24	(a)	31	(c)
4	(a)	11	(a)	18	(c)	25	(b)	32	(d)
5	(c)	12	(d)	19	(c)	26	(d)	33	(b)
6	(a)	13	(a)	20	(b)	27	(a)	34	(b)
7	(d)	14	(b)	21	(b)	28	(c)	35	(d)

1. (c) Number comes between 19 and 21 is 20.

2. (b) Arun has balloons = 10

Varun has balloons = 7

Now, 10 − 7 = 3

So, Arun has 3 balloons more than Varun.

3. (b) June is the sixth month of the year.

4. (a) The height of tree = 7 units

5. (c) 6 ice-creams + 3 ice-creams = 9 ice-creams.

6. (a) Apples = 4

Oranges = 3

Total fruits = 4 + 3 = 7

7. (d) From figure 9 − 3 = 6

8 − 2 = 6

6 + 0 = 6

2 + 4 = 6

3 + 3 = 6

8. (c) Bees in the beehive = 19

Bees flew away = 12

Bees left = 19 − 12 = 7

9. (b) Neelam has roses = 10

She gives to her friend = 3

Roses left to her = 10 − 3 = 7

7 roses are left to her.

10. (c) An envelope has rectangular shape. Ball is spherical, clock is circular and dice is cubic.

11. (a) Circle will come in the blank in the pattern.

12. (d) Birthday cap → Cone

Football → Sphere

Cold drink can → Cylinder

Book → Cuboid

13. (a) 1 Tens = 10

7 Ones = + 7 = 17

Total lily flowers = 17.

14. (b) 86 > 65 > 32 > 24 > 12

15. (d) Sunday is the last day of week. First day of week is Monday.

16. (c) Santa Claus comes to town riding on his sleigh in December.

17. (b) Arjun has,

₹ 10 + ₹ 10 + ₹ 20 + ₹ 5 + ₹ 5 + ₹ 2 + ₹ 2 + ₹ 1 + ₹ 1 + ₹ 1 + ₹ 1 = ₹ 58

18. (c) ₹ 10 is available in both note and coin.

Coin of ₹ 10   Note of ₹ 10

19. (c) Bag (a) has = ₹ 20

Bag (b) has = ₹ 10 + ₹ 5 + ₹ 5 = ₹ 20

Bag (c) has = ₹ 100

Bag (d) has = ₹ 10 + ₹ 20 + ₹ 5 = ₹ 35

Bag (c) has more money than bag (a), bag (b) and bag (d).

20. (b) $7 + 7 + 7 + 7 + 7 + 7 = 6 \times 7 = 42$

21. (b) Number of girls = 24

Number of boys = 28

Total Students = 24 + 28 = 52

22. (b) 3 tens and 4 ones = 34

= Thirty four

23. (b) (arrow) is not made up of curved lines. It is made up of 7 straight lines.

24. (a) Parrots sitting on the tree = 24

Parrots come and sit on the tree = 4

Total parrots on the tree = 24 + 4 = 28

Now, there are 28 parrots sitting on the tree.

25. (b) $7 - 0 = 7$

26. (d) Here, 15

$1 + 5 = 6$

15 is less than 20.

27. (a) 3 bunches of ten grapes each = 3 tens

5 loose grapes = 5 ones

Total grapes = 3 tens + 5 ones = 35

28. (c) Number of big fishes = 40

Number of small fishes = 26

Total number of fishes = 40 + 26 = 66

So, there are 66 fishes in all.

29. (c) Feather is lightest among given objects.

30. (b) Hour hand is at 6

and minute hand is at 12

Time shown by clock = 6 o'clock.

31. (c) There are 8 cars on the road.

32. (d) There are

Number of Autos = 2

Number of Buses = 3

Number of Trucks = 6

Number of Bikes = 5

Number of cars = 8

Number of Autos is least on the road.

33. (b) Number of trucks = 6

Number of buses = 3

So,   6 − 3 = 3

There are 3 trucks more on the road than buses.

34. (b) $9 < 17 < 20$

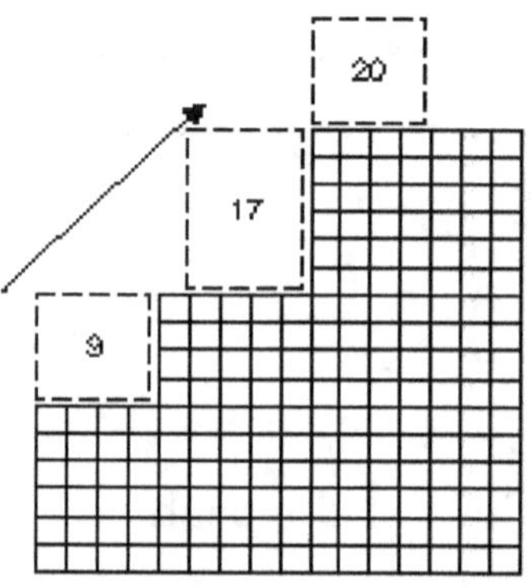

35. (d) $96 = 90 + 6$

= Ninety-Six

MOCK TEST 4

ANSWER KEY

1	(d)	8	(a)	15	(d)	22	(c)	29	(b)
2	(c)	9	(a)	16	(c)	23	(a)	30	(c)
3	(b)	10	(d)	17	(b)	24	(b)	31	(d)
4	(a)	11	(c)	18	(a)	25	(d)	32	(d)
5	(c)	12	(d)	19	(b)	26	(b)	33	(c)
6	(d)	13	(a)	20	(d)	27	(a)	34	(d)
7	(a)	14	(b)	21	(b)	28	(a)	35	(a)

1. (d) Seventy nine can be written as 70 + 9.

2. (c) 4 tens and 2 ones is equal to 42.

T	O
4	2

3. (b) A bottle holds more milk than glass, cup and spoon.

4. (a) 4 + 4 = 8

44 is greater than 8

5. (c) Number of green balloons = 13

Number of orange balloons = 2

Number of red balloons = 3

Total number of balloons = 13 + 2 + 3 = 18

6. (d) Number of bananas = 3

Number of apples = 5

Number of oranges = 6

Total number of fruits = 3 + 5 + 6 = 14

7. (a) Frogs counted by Nikita = 12

Frogs jumped out = 5

Frogs left = 12 – 5 = 7

8. (a) Number of zebras = 10

Number of elephants = 13

Number of tigers = 15

Total number of animals in the zoo = 10 + 13 + 15 = 38

9. (a) Total number of chocolates = 18

Number of chocolates eaten by Ravi = 3

Number of chocolates left = 18 – 3 = 15

10. (d) Number of students in class 4 = 45

Students absent on Wednesday = 8

Students present on Wednesday = 45 – 8 = 37

11. (c) The length of the scale is about 7 eraser long.

12. (d) 12

13. (a) ₹ 5 is available in both note and coin.

14.(b) The minute hand is at 12 and the hour hand is at 8. Therefore, the time is 8 : 00.

15.(d) The number of days between Monday and Thursday is 2, i.e, Tuesday and Wednesday.

16.(c) Today is Wednesday, then yesterday was Tuesday.

17.(b) A - 2, B - 1, C - 4, D - 3.

18.(a) Only book slides among all the given objects.

19.(b) The number line shows 5 + 3.

20.(d) The fruit basket is kept on the table.

21.(b) Total Number of fruit cakes = 69
Fruit cakes given to friends = 25
Fruit cakes left with her =
69 − 25 = 44

22.(c) Price of a pencil box = ₹ 15
Price of two pencil boxes =
15 + 15 = ₹ 30

23.(a) Rectangle is a flat shape.

24.(b) Total amount of money
= ₹ 50 + ₹ 10 + ₹ 5 + ₹ 5 + ₹ 2
= ₹ 72

25.(d) June comes just after fifth month which is May.

26.(b) As it is shown in the table, Nitin got only one star which is least of all.

27.(a) Abhishek got 5 stars.

28.(a) Shreya got 4 stars.

29.(b) There are 5 students in class 2 who got stars.

30.(c) Total numbers of eggs = 24 eggs
Number of broken eggs = 4
Number of eggs that were in good condition = 24 − 4 = 20 eggs.

31.(d) Cylinder is a solid shape.

32.(d) Total money that Rajat has = ₹ 50
Price of the motor bike = ₹ 75
More amount required by Rajat to purchase the motor bike
= ₹ 75 − ₹ 50 = ₹ 25

33.(c) will come next in the pattern.

34.(d) 17 < 29 < 34

35.(a) When 5 is added to 24 then it will become 29.
24 + 5 = 29

MOCK TEST 5

ANSWER KEY

1	(a)	8	(b)	15	(c)	22	(a)	29	(c)
2	(b)	9	(c)	16	(c)	23	(b)	30	(a)
3	(a)	10	(a)	17	(b)	24	(c)	31	(a)
4	(a)	11	(b)	18	(a)	25	(b)	32	(b)
5	(c)	12	(a)	19	(c)	26	(a)	33	(a)
6	(b)	13	(a)	20	(a)	27	(a)	34	(d)
7	(d)	14	(a)	21	(c)	28	(b)	35	(d)

1. **(a)** The number are increasing by adding 2.

   $2 + 2 = 4$

   $4 + 2 = 6$

   $6 + 2 = 8$

   $8 + 2 = 10$

   $10 + 2 = 12.$

2. **(b)** 24 comes between 23 and 25.

3. **(a)** September comes before October.

4. **(a)** Hour hand is at 5 and minute hand is at 12. So, its 5 o' clock.

5. **(c)** A. Ice-cream $\rightarrow$ 4. Cone

   B. Ball $\rightarrow$ 3. Sphere

   C. Chocolate $\rightarrow$ 1. Cuboid

   D. Coke $\rightarrow$ 2. Cylinder

6. **(b)** Rat is inside the house and cat is outside the house.

7. **(d)** 3 apples + 4 apples = 7 apples

8. **(b)** $12 + 8 = 20$

9. **(c)** Book

10. **(a)** 15 toffees + 2 apples = 17

11. **(b)** 15 toffees − 4 toffees = 11 toffees.

12. **(a)** $24 + 15 = 39$

13. **(a)** 12, A cow has 4 legs. $4 + 4 + 4 = 12.$

14. **(a)** Number of heads of cows = 3

    Number of heads of hens = 5

    Total heads = 8

15. **(c)** Total number of flowers = 64

    Number of flowers used = 35

    Number of flowers left

    $= 64 - 35 = 29$

16. **(c)** $5 + 5 + 5 + 5 + 5 + 5 + 5 = 7 \times 5$

17. **(b)** Thursday

18. **(a)** There are seven frogs in the picture.

19. **(c)** There are five birds in the picture.

20. **(a)** There are eight butterflies in the picture.

21. **(c)**

22. **(a)** There are 2 boys on left side and right side has 1 boy only. So, left side is heavier than right side.

23. **(b)**

24. **(c)** Will come next in the pattern.

25. **(b)** ₹ 20,

$₹ 10 + ₹ 5 + ₹ 5 = ₹ 20$

26. **(a)** $20 - 7 = 13$

27. **(a)** $14 - 11 = 3$

    Bowl 1 has 3 marbles more than Bowl 2.

28. **(b)** 59, 47, 33, 25, 12

29. **(c)** 4, Four straight lines.

30. **(a)** G

31. **(a)** This jug holds 5 cups of water.

32. **(b)** $9 < 23 < 44 < 77 < 93$

33. **(a)** January

34. **(d)** April

35. **(d)** 3 students

SCIENCE

MOCK TEST 1

ANSWER KEY

1	(d)	8	(c)	15	(b)	22	(d)	29	(b)
2	(d)	9	(b)	16	(c)	23	(b)	30	(d)
3	(c)	10	(a)	17	(d)	24	(c)	31	(c)
4	(b)	11	(b)	18	(c)	25	(c)	32	(c)
5	(d)	12	(b)	19	(d)	26	(c)	33	(d)
6	(a)	13	(b)	20	(d)	27	(a)	34	(c)
7	(d)	14	(c)	21	(c)	28	(d)	35	(d)

1. **(d)** Tiger can move from one place to another on its own as it is a living thing.

2. **(d)** All of these (air, water, sunlight) are necessary for the growth of a plant.

3. **(c)** A stone does not need air, water and food for its growth.

4. **(b)** We use to wear sweater in winter.

5. **(d)** Parrot is a bird.

6. **(a)** Mango is called the king of fruits.

7. **(d)** Vegetables and fruits are nutritious food.

8. **(c)** Ant is an insect.

9. **(b)** Frog eats insect.

10. **(a)** We obtained food grains from plants.

11. **(b)** Always cross the road using zebra crossing.

12. **(b)** Rice

13. **(b)** Chilli is green in colour and spicy.

14. **(c)** The home of horse is known as stable.

15. **(b)** Ostrich cannot fly.

16. **(c)** Ear helps to hear a bell.

17. **(d)** House keeps us safe from heat, rain and wild animals.

18. **(c)** Summer days are hot, winter days are cold. A strong wind blows on windy day and monsoon days are rainy.

19. **(d)** Carpenter makes furniture and plumber repairs pipes at our home.

20. **(d)** Uncle and wife both are considered as family members.

21. **(c)** Mango contains one seed only.

22. **(d)** Tree is a living thing.

23. **(b)** Air has weight.

24. **(c)** Food protects our body from diseases.

25. **(c)** A — 3, B — 4, C — 2, D — 1

26. **(c)** A — 3, B — 1, C — 2, D — 4

27.(a) Doctor works in hospitals.

28.(d) Independence day is a national festival.

29.(b) Moon changes its shape every night.

30.(d) Cycle does not have engines and are not pulled by animals.

It is pulled by manpower.

31.(c) Tyres are made up of rubber.

32.(c) Rocket is man-made.

33.(d) Toy robot will remain same after 1 year.

34.(c) Planes will fly in the clouds.

35.(d) Shark is found in oceans.

MOCK TEST 2

ANSWER KEY

1	(a)	8	(d)	15	(c)	22	(d)	29	(d)
2	(a)	9	(b)	16	(d)	23	(c)	30	(a)
3	(d)	10	(a)	17	(d)	24	(b)	31	(a)
4	(a)	11	(c)	18	(b)	25	(b)	32	(d)
5	(c)	12	(d)	19	(c)	26	(a)	33	(d)
6	(b)	13	(b)	20	(d)	27	(d)	34	(c)
7	(d)	14	(c)	21	(c)	28	(d)	35	(b)

1. (c) Banyan tree is the national tree.

2. (a) Policeman catches thieves.

3. (d) Eye is a sense organ.

4. (a) A — 3, B — 1, C — 4, D — 2

5. (c) Policeman does not help in the construction of a house.

6. (b) Train is a non-living thing used for travelling.

7. (d) Penguin is a bird which cannot fly. It is a flightless bird.

8. (d) Both Spinach and Peas are green in colour.

9. (b) Blade is not made up of plastic.

10.(a) We must wash our hands after and before eating food.

11.(c) We like to sit near table fan when we feel hot.

12.(d) All of these are family members.

13.(b) Tomato is a fruit.

14.(c) A — 3, B — 4, C — 1, D— 2

15.(c) Green light says 'go'.

16.(d) Tomato and cucumber are used to prepare salad.

17.(d) Temple, Church and Mosque are all places of worship.

18.(b) It is a tailor, who stiches clothes.

19.(c) Both are insects.

20.(d) Stones are non-living.

21.(c) Water is the common thing that is required for cooking, washing, bathing and planting a tree.

22.(d) Both raincoat and umbrella protect us from rain.

23. (c) Bus can move from one place to another.

24. (b) Dolphin is a water animal.

25. (b) Teacher teaches us many subjects in a school.

26. (a) The gardener looks after the school garden.

27. (d) On 2nd October, we celebrate the birthday of Gandhi ji which is popularly known as Gandhi Jayanti.

28. (d) Crackers are used in diwali. Coloured water and colours (Gulal) are used to play holi.

29. (d) Activity A, B and C are dangerous.

30. (a) Head is a body part.

31. (a) Nose is not in pair. Nose is one in number.

32. (d) We brush our teeth in the bathroom.

33. (d) They all are birds.

34. (c) Girls shirt is made up of threads of cotton.

35. (b) Apple is a fruit, maize corn is a food grain , rose is used in perfume and wood is used in making furniture.

MOCK TEST 3

ANSWER KEY

1	(b)	8	(a)	15	(d)	22	(a)	29	(b)
2	(d)	9	(a)	16	(c)	23	(d)	30	(b)
3	(b)	10	(d)	17	(b)	24	(b)	31	(c)
4	(d)	11	(a)	18	(a)	25	(d)	32	(d)
5	(d)	12	(a)	19	(c)	26	(d)	33	(c)
6	(c)	13	(b)	20	(b)	27	(a)	34	(a)
7	(d)	14	(b)	21	(d)	28	(a)	35	(b)

1. (b) Neem tree is a living thing.

2. (d) (II) Clean your hands first.
(III) Wash the fruits.
(I) Cut them safely with knife.
(IV) Eat the fruits as they keep us healthy.

3. (b) Heart is present in chest.

4. (d) A bulb is not made up of plastic. It is made up of glass.

5. (d) We get wood, fruits and pulses from plants.

6. (c) One who gives milk is cow and the one which is used for travelling from one place to another is horse.

7. (d) Hat is used to protect head.

8. (a) Air is the common thing that a kite as well as a person needs.

9. (a) Cycle can be used only for 2 people. If 4 people want to move together then car can be used. Aeroplane and train are used for many number of people.

10. (d) Burning fire crackers make air dirty, create lot of noise and are harmful for us.

11. (a) Doctor helps us by giving medicine when we have high fever and stomach pain.

12. (a) Wait for your turn.

13. (b) You should use soap while washing dirty hands.

14. (b) Woollen clothes are used in winters.

15. (d) Dog and rabbit are pet animals kids love to play with them. Giraffe is not a pet animal.

16. (c) Cucumber is not a fruit. It is a vegetable.

17. (b) Plants cannot move from one place to another.

18. (a) Tailor makes your school uniform.

19. (c) Apply dettol on the injured area to avoid infection

20. (b) Mother of our father is our grandmother.

21. (d) Human body is made up of different organs, sense organs and systems.

22. (a) Parrot is green in colour and eats green chilly.

23. (d) Ship and Train do not run on the road. Ship moves in water and train runs on railway tracks.

24. (b) Flower is the most beautiful part of a plant.

25. (d) All of these animals live in the forest.

26. (d) Aeroplane can be used to travel in the air.

27. (a) People living near our house are neighbours.

28. (a) Skin helps us to feel things.

29. (b) Diwali

30. (b) Parrot is kept as a pet.

31. (c) Diwali is the festival of lights.

32. (d) In the spring and autumn season, weather is neither hot nor cold.

33. (c) Brick is used to build pucca house. Mud, straw and bamboo is used to make kutcha house.

34. (a) Herbivores

35. (b) Birds live in nests.

MOCK TEST 4

ANSWER KEY

1	(d)	9	(b)	17	(a)	25	(d)	33	(b)
2	(c)	10	(d)	18	(c)	26	(d)	34	(d)
3	(d)	11	(c)	19	(b)	27	(c)	35	(c)
4	(c)	12	(d)	20	(b)	28	(c)	36	(b)
5	(a)	13	(a)	21	(b)	29	(b)	37	(c)
6	(d)	14	(b)	22	(b)	30	(b)	38	(a)
7	(b)	15	(b)	23	(b)	31	(d)	39	(a)
8	(b)	16	(b)	24	(a)	32	(d)	40	(c)

1. **(d)** Tea, coffee and sugar come from plants.

2. **(c)** Both the statements are correct.

3. **(d)** Dolphin and blue whale both are water animals.

4. **(c)** Rabbit eats grass.

5. **(a)** Non-living thing does not move, die and breathe

6. **(d)** Husband and wife are family members. Cousins are member of big or joint family.

7. **(b)** We post our letters in post-office.

8. **(b)** Yellow light indicates wait.

9. **(b)** We should not play with scissord.

10. **(d)** Police help to catch thieves.

11. **(c)** Earth

12. **(d)** Rabindra Nath Tagore

13. **(a)** Aeroplane is the fastest and most expensive mode of transportation.

14. **(b)** The relationship between Lalita and Raghav is mother-son.

15. **(b)** Sunglasses are made up of glass.

16. **(b)** Bedroom

17. **(a)** Vultures feed on dead animals.

18. **(c)** Hen lays eggs. Lion and deer give birth to young ones.

19. **(b)** A - 3, B - 1, C - 4, D - 2

20. **(b)** Ear is used in listening music, eye is used to watch a bird. We taste the ice-cream by tongue.

21. **(b)** Mobile phone is best way to communicate with uncle Sam in Australia.

22. **(b)** Brinjal can be eaten only after cooking.

23. **(b)** Brain is a part of nervous system.

24. **(a)** Very small plants are called herbs.

25. **(d)** Mosquito and ant are insects, parrot is a bird.

26. **(d)** Spoon is non-living thing.

27. **(c)** Climbers need the support to grow.

28. **(c)** Nose is not present in pair.

29. **(b)** Tiger is a wild animal and frog lives on land as well as water.

30. **(b)** Pumpkin is a vegetable, pineapple is a fruit, wheat is a grain, guava is a fruit.

31. **(d)** Horse lives in stable.

32. **(d)**

33. **(b)** Water conservation means reducing the use of water.

34. **(d)** All the statements are true.

35. **(c)** Mother of your father is called 'grandmother'.

36. **(b)** Frog eats insects.

37. **(a)** Eyes help us to read a book

38. **(c)** Milk keeps our bones and teeth healthy.

39. **(a)** For lighting a fire, air is necessary.

40. **(c)** On a cold day, we like to have hot coffee.

MOCK TEST 5

ANSWER KEY

1	(b)	9	(d)	17	(b)	25	(b)	33	(a)
2	(a)	10	(a)	18	(d)	26	(d)	34	(c)
3	(d)	11	(d)	19	(b)	27	(b)	35	(b)
4	(c)	12	(d)	20	(d)	28	(a)	36	(c)
5	(c)	13	(a)	21	(c)	29	(a)	37	(c)
6	(a)	14	(d)	22	(a)	30	(b)	38	(a)
7	(d)	15	(b)	23	(a)	31	(a)	39	(b)
8	(a)	16	(b)	24	(d)	32	(a)	40	(b)

1. **(b)** Temple, Gurudwara and Mosque are places of worship. School is the place of education.

2. **(a)** Monkey is an animal which can be found in a forest, jumping on the trees.

3. **(d)** Both car and bus are non-living things.

4. **(c)** Cat needs air to breathe.

5. **(c)** Humans, animals and plants are living things and food is a non-living thing.

6. **(a)** She is Mother Teresa.

7. **(d)** Heater, sweater and gloves are used in winters and skirt is used to wear in summer.

8. **(a)** Christmas is celebrated by Christians and Republic day is celebrated by all Indians.

9. **(d)** Do not use shower for bathing. This will waste a lot of water. Use bucket for bathing.

10. **(a)** Peacock is a bird, octopus is a water animal, insect can fly and sheep is an animal.

11. **(d)** Children of uncles and aunts are called cousins.

12. **(d)** Food makes us strong and healthy.

13. **(a)** Tongue is red in colour.

14. **(d)** A - 4, B - 1, C - 2, D - 3

15. **(b)** Milk is needed by a human body to grow.

16. **(b)** Never touch electric switches and plugs with wet hands, it may give you an electric shock.

17. **(b)** Fallen leaves are non-living thing.

18. **(d)** Nose is an external part of the human body. Heart, Brain and Lungs are present inside the body.

19.(b) People in villages use bullock carts to travel from one place to another.

20.(d) Birthday and marriage, both are family occasion.

21.(c) You do not see airports usually in your neighbourhood.

22.(a) Fireman does not sell milk. He puts off the fire.

23.(a) Wheat is a food grain which is used to make chapatti.

24.(d) Licking of finger is not a good habit.

25.(b) After it rains we see a rainbow up in the sky.

26.(d) A weather can be windy, rainy or hot but not sweet.

27.(b) we get milk from animals.

28.(a) A - 4, B - 1, C - 2, D - 3.

29.(a) Flower changes into fruits.

30.(b) Water is the common thing that a ship, a fish and a plant needs.

Ship needs water to move, fish and plant needs water to grow.

31.(a) Barber will help you to get a new hairstyle.

32.(a) We should look left and right before crossing the road.

33.(a) Ram and Rohan are brothers. Mrs. Geeta is their mother.

34.(c) In picture 1, a person is using water for cooking food

In picture 2, a person is using water for washing clothes.

35.(b) The meal which we eat in the afternoon is called lunch.

36.(c) Farmer grow crops in the field.

37.(c) A kutcha house is mostly found in villages.

38.(a) Gandhi Jayanti is a national festival celebrated by all Indians.

39.(b) Vulture

40.(b) Birds nest in trees but owl lives in tree holes as well as in the ground holes.

GENERAL KNOWLEDGE

MOCK TEST 1

ANSWER KEY									
1	(b)	6	(a)	11	(a)	16	(b)	21	(b)
2	(a)	7	(c)	12	(c)	17	(c)	22	(b)
3	(c)	8	(b)	13	(d)	18	(b)	23	(b)
4	(b)	9	(a)	14	(c)	19	(d)	24	(c)
5	(a)	10	(b)	15	(c)	20	(a)	25	(b)

1. **(b)** Pharmacy refers to a shop or hospital dispensary where medicinal drugs are prepared or sold.

2. **(a)** An astronaut is a person who is trained to travel in a spacecraft.

3. **(c)** Holi is an Indian festival celebrated in India and Nepal, also known as the "festival of colours".

4. **(b)** The Gateway of India is an arch monument built during the 20th century in Mumbai, India.

5. **(a)** The Bengal Tiger was declared as the national animal of India in April 1973.

6. **(a)** A gurdwara (meaning "door to the Guru") is a place of worship for Sikhs.

7. **(c)** Lotus is the National Flower of India. It is a sacred flower and occupies a unique position in the art and mythology of ancient India.

8. **(b)** Father of the Nation is a title given to Mahatma Gandhi who was considered the driving force behind India's independence.

9. **(a)** With a length of 2525 km (1569 miles), The Ganges or Ganga is the longest river in India.

10. **(b)** An aquatic animal is an animal which lives in water for most or all of its life.

11. **(a)** Dr. Rajendra Prasad was elected as the nation's first President.

12. **(c)** P.V. Sindhu is an Indian badminton player who became the first Indian woman to win an Olympic silver medal at Olympics.

13. **(d)** **Wolf** or grey wolf is found in the wild and remote areas.

14. **(c)** Lion is a wild animal.

15. **(c)** The Red Fort is a historical fort in the city of Delhi in India.

16. **(b)** New Delhi is the capital of India.

19. **(d)** **Vir**at Kohli is currently the captain of the Indian national team.

20. **(a)** Ram Nath Kovind is an Indian lawyer and politician who has been elected the President of India.

21. **(b)** Popeye eats spinach to become strong.

25. **(b)** Animals that eat meat are called carnivores.

MOCK TEST 2

ANSWER KEY

1	(c)	6	(b)	11	(c)	16	(d)	21	(b)
2	(a)	7	(b)	12	(a)	17	(b)	22	(c)
3	(b)	8	(d)	13	(c)	18	(c)	23	(a)
4	(b)	9	(b)	14	(c)	19	(b)	24	(d)
5	(a)	10	(c)	15	(d)	20	(d)	25	(a)

1. (c) Christmas is not a national festival.

2. (a) The image is of Santa Claus who is said to bring gifts for children on Christmas.

3. (b) Mahatma Gandhi is also known as 'Bapu'.

4. (b) Pen

5. (a) Apple Inc. is the name of an American company that sells computer software.

6. (b) Gurpurab is celebration of an anniversary related to the lives of the Sikh gurus.

7. (b) Nurses are health care professionals who take care of patients.

8. (d) A blacksmith is a person who makes iron and steel tools.

10. (c) Everest is a mountain.

11. (c) Mary Kom is an Indian boxer.

12. (b) Vande Mataram is the national song of India. It was originally composed in Bengali by poet Bankim Chandra Chatterji.

13. (c) Dr. Rajendra Prasad was the first President of the Republic of India.

14. (c) The tailed aquatic larva of a frog is called tadpole.

15. (d) A stable is a place for horses which is divided into separate stalls for each horse.

16. (d) A glove is a covering for the hands; worn for protection against cold or dirt and typically having separate parts for each finger and the thumb.

19. (b) Pluto is the pet and friend of Mickey Mouse.

20. (d) Ram Nath Kovind is the 14th and current President of India.

21. (b) For calling a police you can dial 100.

22. (c) Chimpanzees are the species of the great apes which are mammals.

23. (a) The sun cannot be observed at night.

24. (d) There are 29 states in India.

25. (a) Vatican City is the smallest country in the world.

MOCK TEST 3

ANSWER KEY									
1	(a)	**6**	(a)	**11**	(a)	**16**	(c)	**21**	(b)
2	(c)	**7**	(a)	**12**	(b)	**17**	(c)	**22**	(b)
3	(c)	**8**	(b)	**13**	(b)	**18**	(c)	**23**	(b)
4	(a)	**9**	(a)	**14**	(c)	**19**	(b)	**24**	(b)
5	(a)	**10**	(d)	**15**	(b)	**20**	(c)	**25**	(c)

1. (a) Pulse Polio is an immunization campaign by the government to eliminate polio in India by vaccinating all children under the age of five years against the polio virus.

2. (c) Camels are known as the ship of the desert because they can move across desert sands easily.

3. (c) February is the shortest month of the year as it is the only month to have a length of less than 30 days. The month has 28 days in common years or 29 days in leap years.

4. (a) Hindi is the official Language of India.

5. (a) Blue whale is the largest animal in the world.

6. (a) Asia is the largest continent in the world.

7. (a) One hundred years make a century.

8. (b) The Qutub Minar, is a monument located in New Delhi.

9. (a) A laptop is a type of computer which can be carried from one place to another.

10. (d) **Rus**sia is the largest country in the world having area of 17.1 million km².

11. (a) Seviyan is a special dish made during Eid-ul-Fitr.

12. (b) February has 28 days in common years or 29 days in leap years.

13. (b) Dussehra is a Hindu festival of India to celebrate the victory of good over evil.

14. (c) Christmas is celebrated on 25th December.

15. (b) Cow is a domestic animal; other options show wild animals.

16. (c) An aeroplane carries many people to far off places.

17. (c) The ostrich is the tallest and the heaviest bird. It does not fly but it runs fast.

18. (c) Penguins are a group of aquatic, flightless birds. They live almost exclusively in cold climates, such as Antarctica.

19. (b) Amitabh Bachchan is known as Big B.

20. (c) Gold is a movie based on life of a hockey player Dhyanchand.

21. (b) Currently Donald Trump is the president of United States of America.

22. (b) An ambulance moves with a siren.

23. (b) Potatoes are rich in carbohydrates and give energy to our body.

24. (b) The earth is also called the blue planet.

MOCK TEST 4

ANSWER KEY

1	(b)	9	(a)	17	(b)	25	(a)	33	(d)
2	(b)	10	(b)	18	(a)	26	(a)	34	(a)
3	(d)	11	(a)	19	(b)	27	(a)	35	(b)
4	(c)	12	(c)	20	(b)	28	(a)	36	(d)
5	(b)	13	(a)	21	(a)	29	(a)	37	(b)
6	(c)	14	(b)	22	(a)	30	(c)	38	(c)
7	(c)	15	(b)	23	(a)	31	(d)	39	(c)
8	(d)	16	(c)	24	(d)	32	(b)	40	(b)

1. **(b)** Bees produce honey and store it in wax structures called honeycombs.
2. **(b)** Rhinoceros are characterized by their size, thick protective skin and a large horn.
3. **(d)** **Sna**kes are elongated, legless, carnivorous reptiles.
4. **(c)** Baby of a goat is called kid.
5. **(b)** Baby of a deer is called fawn.
6. **(c)** The lion lives in a den.
7. **(c)** Sheep is a mammal; others are birds.
8. **(d)** **Ba**by of a kangaroo is called joey.
9. **(a)** The dog lives in a kennel.
10. **(b)** Sound made by a pig is called oink.
11. **(a)** Mercury is the closest planet to the Sun so it is the hottest planet.
12. **(c)** Jupiter is the largest planet.
13. **(a)** Sachin Tendulkar is also known as the 'Master Blaster'.
14. **(b)** Milkha Singh is also known as the 'Flying Sikh'.
15. **(b)** Tennis is played at Wimbledon.
16. **(c)** The wheel in the Indian flag has 24 spokes.
17. **(b)** National Anthem of India was written by Rabindranath Tagore.
18. **(a)** Jawaharlal Nehru was the 1st Prime Minister of India
19. **(b)** Sarojini Naidu is known as the Nightingale of India
20. **(b)** A caterpillar comes out of the egg of a butterfly.
21. **(a)** Head, thorax and abdomen are the 3 main body parts of a butterfly.
22. **(c)** Butterflies have 6 legs.
23. **(a)** The Sun is the nearest star to planet Earth.
24. **(d)** **Legs** are not sense organs. The nose, skin, eyes, ears and tongue are sense organs.
25. **(a)** Cheetah is the fastest animal on the land.
26. **(a)** Our skin is the most sensitive part of our body.
27. **(a)** The Sun is the principal source of energy for Earth.

28. (a) The two holes in the nose are called nostrils.

29. (a) The Nile is the longest river on the earth.

30. (c) Apart from water, fruit and fibre, coconut also give us oil.

31. (d) Tomato is a fruit.

32. (b) The hard part inside our body is called bone.

33. (d) Most widely spoken language in the world is Chinese.

34. (a) Bhangra is the folk dance of Punjab.

35. (b) Banyan is the National tree of India.

36. (d) Subhash Chandra Bose was popularly known as Netaji.

37. (b) Snow white was poisoned by an apple by the evil queen who came as an old woman.

38. (c) A rainbow has seven colours violet, indigo, blue, green, yellow, orange and red. Silver colour is not present in a rainbow.

39. (c) The baby of a zebra is called a colt.

40. (b) The sentence is in the past tense, so use of 'was' is grammatically correct.

MOCK TEST 5

ANSWER KEY

1	(a)	9	(c)	17	(b)	25	(d)	33	(d)
2	(c)	10	(b)	18	(b)	26	(c)	34	(d)
3	(c)	11	(c)	19	(b)	27	(c)	35	(a)
4	(c)	12	(b)	20	(d)	28	(c)	36	(c)
5	(c)	13	(c)	21	(a)	29	(c)	37	(b)
6	(d)	14	(b)	22	(a)	30	(b)	38	(b)
7	(b)	15	(c)	23	(a)	31	(b)	39	(b)
8	(d)	16	(a)	24	(b)	32	(b)	40	(d)

MOCK TEST - 5

1. (a) Hummingbird is the smallest bird in the world.

2. (c) Giraffe is the tallest animal in the world

3. (c) Ostrich is the largest bird in the world

4. (c) Igloo is made up of ice.

5. (c) There are five vowels, a,e,i,o,u.

6. (d) Saturn

7. (b) Mercury is the fastest moving planet.

8. (d) Sahara desert is the largest desert in the world.

9. (c) Pacific ocean is the largest ocean in the world.

10.(b) Mount Everest is the highest mountain peak in the world.

11.(c) Japan is also called 'Land of the Rising Sun'.

12.(b) Taj Mahal was built by Shah Jahan in memory of his wife Mumtaz Mahal.

13.(c) We wear warm clothes in winter.

14.(b) An egg is oval in shape.

15.(c) There are 366 days in a leap year.

16.(a) There is only one mouth in our body.

17.(b) A mosque is the place of worship for Muslims.

18.(b) Baby of a horse is called colt.

19.(b) There are three colours-saffron, white and green in our national flag.

20.(d) Neil Armstrong was the first person to land on moon.

21.(a) Teacher's Day is celebrated on 5th September.

22.(a) Kiwi bird is the national bird of New Zealand.

23.(a) Rupess 5 is equal to 500 paise.

24.(b) A person who plays music is called a musician.

25.(d) Full form of P.T.O. is Please Turn Over.

26.(c) Gir National Park in Gujarat is famous for lion.

27.(c) Dams are built to control flood.

28.(c) There are 26 letters in English alphabet.

29.(c) Cataract is a disease of eyes.

30.(b) Camel has hump on its back.

31.(b) There are 206 bones in our body.

32.(b) An adult human has 32 teeth.

33.(d) There are 11 players in a hockey team.

34.(d) Cactus grows in desert regions.

35.(a) Ghee is made from milk.

36.(c) Except aeroplane all other means of transport move on land.

37.(b) A figure with 3 sides is called a triangle.

38.(b) Agra is situated on the bank of river Yamuna.

39.(b) A place where fish are kept is called an aquarium.

40.(d) Internet is used for e-mail, chatting, surfing and a number of other applications.

LOGICAL REASONING

MOCK TEST 1

	ANSWER KEY								
1	(a)	7	(c)	13	(b)	19	(c)	25	(d)
2	(d)	8	(c)	14	(d)	20	(b)	26	(c)
3	(d)	9	(c)	15	(b)	21	(c)	27	(a)
4	(c)	10	(d)	16	(d)	22	(a)	28	(b)
5	(c)	11	(d)	17	(a)	23	(d)	29	(b)
6	(d)	12	(a)	18	(b)	24	(b)	30	(d)

1. **(a)** As, $4 - 1 = 3$, there are three triangles.

   Similarly, $5 - 1 = 4$, there are four squares.

2. **(d)** Top figure becomes bottom figure and bottom figure becomes top.

3. **(d)** Arrows are changing their positions after changing their directions.

4. **(c)** $2 + 2 + 2 + 2 = 8$ muffins. Each child gets 2 muffins.

5. **(c)** Option (c) Figure is same as the figure (X).

6. **(d)** Elephant is in the first position.

7. **(c)** One kitten has 2 ears. Three kittens have $2 + 2 + 2 = 6$ ears.

8. **(c)** Weight of book = 10 balls (units)

   Weight of pencil = 4 balls (units)
   As, O = 1 unit
   So, = 10 – 4 balls (units)

   = 6 balls (units)

   The book is 6 units heavier than pencil.

9. **(c)** 3 apples are in inside the circle and 2 apples are outside the circle.

10. **(d)** Total circles = 6

    3 circles have three parts.

    2 circles have no parts.

Only 1 circles has two parts shown as

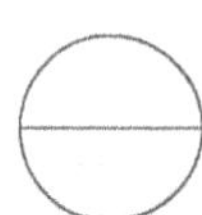

11. (d) Squares = 4

Circles = 4

Stars = 3

Triangles = 5

Hence, triangles are the largest in number.

12. (a)

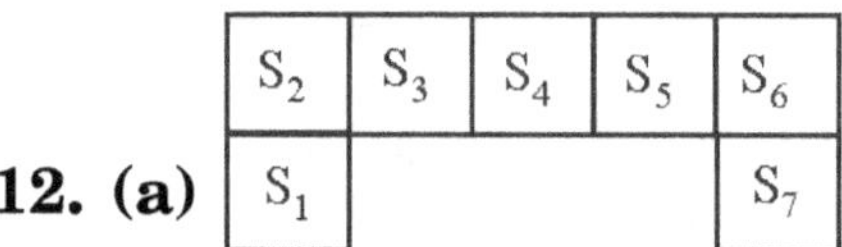

Squares $(S_1, S_2, S_3, S_4, S_5, S_6, S_7) = 7$

13. (b) Pattern is :

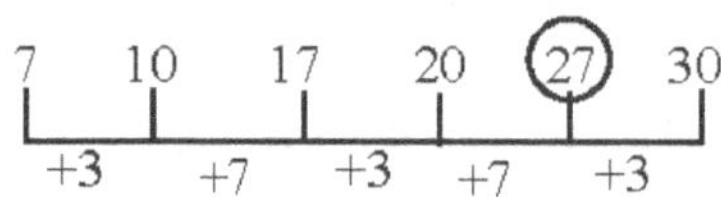

So there will be 7 toffees in the last box.

14. (d) Element in option (d) is different in shape.

15. (b) The number pattern is :

7   10   17   20   (27)   30
  +3   +7   +3   +7   +3

16. (d) Piano, ruler and book have the shape of a rectangle.

17. (a)

18. (b)

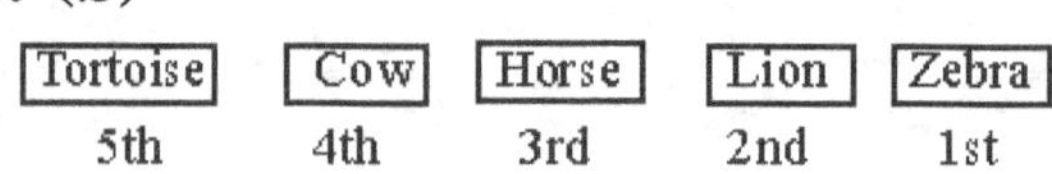

Hence, Zebra comes before lion.

19. (c)

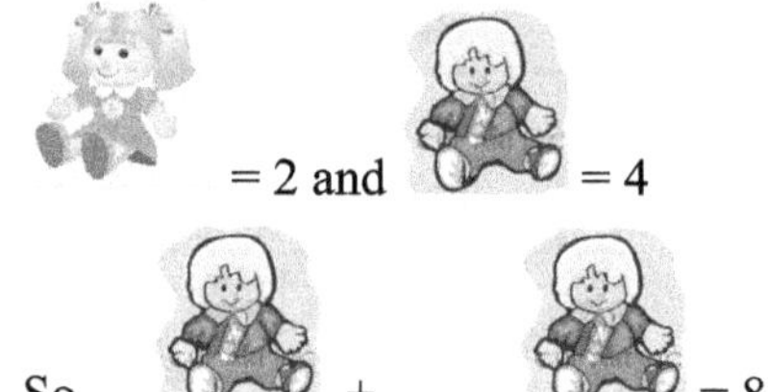

20. (b) Ascending order of Towers :

R < P < Q < S

Tower P is higher than Tower R but lower than Tower Q.

21. (c) Square 1 and square 4 are the same size.

22. (a) Each figure repeats itself after three figures.

23. (d) Bathroom is the smallest room, as it has been shown in the picture.

24. (b)

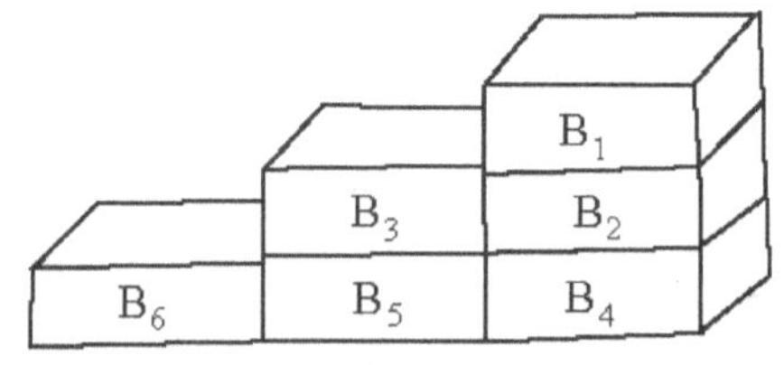

Bricks = $(B_1, B_2, B_3, B_4, B_5, B_6)$

= 6

25. (d) 14 litres of water can be poured into only 16 litres pail.

26. (c) Jyoti's age two years ago = 5 years

Jyoti's present age = 5 + 2 = 7 years

27. (a)

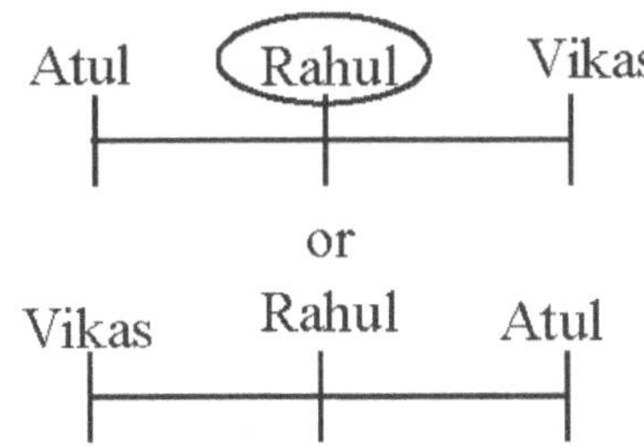

So, Rahul is sitting in the middle.

28. (b) 1 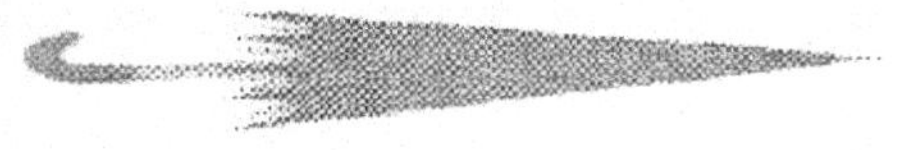 = 1

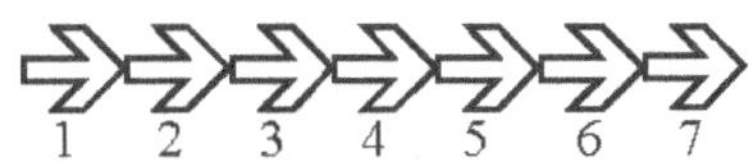

The length of the umbrella is about 7 ⇒ long

29. (b) Figure in option (b) is in the centre of the table.

30. (d) 3 circles and 1 triangles are below the red line.

MOCK TEST 2

ANSWER KEY									
1	(c)	7	(b)	13	(d)	19	(c)	25	(b)
2	(a)	8	(a)	14	(c)	20	(b)	26	(d)
3	(a)	9	(c)	15	(d)	21	(c)	27	(c)
4	(b)	10	(c)	16	(a)	22	(c)	28	(c)
5	(b)	11	(c)	17	(b)	23	(b)	29	(c)
6	(d)	12	(a)	18	(d)	24	(d)	30	(b)

1. **(c)** Each row/column contains four different shapes.

Shape ◯ is missing in fourth row and second column.

2. **(a)** 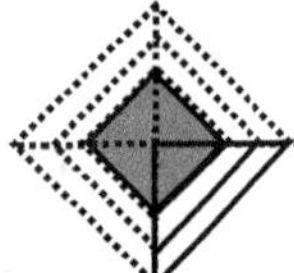

3. **(a)** Length of tape C = 2 units

Length of tape D = 4 units

Tape C is 2 units shorter than tape D.

4. **(b)** 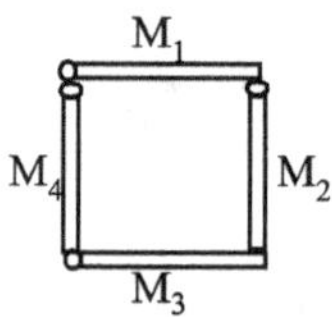

Matchsticks = (M1, M2, M3, M4)

= 4

5. **(b)** Elements in (a), (c) and (d) have same number of lines as in the boundary.

6. **(d)** Ashima is standing nearest to the principal's room door.

7. **(b)** Naksh is standing farthest from the principal's room door.

8. **(a)** 4 flowers are inside the vase.

9. **(c)**

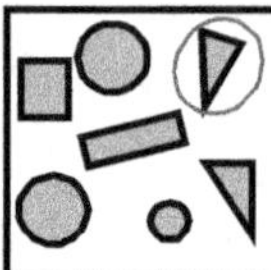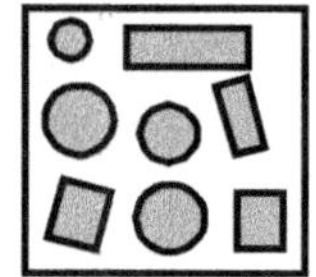

10. **(c)**

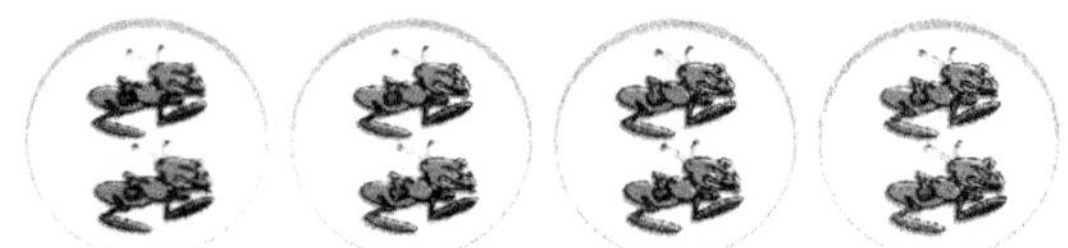

11. **(c)** As in left pair of the figure O is replaced by D and D is replaced by O and vice-versa.

12. **(a)** Tom is just before Beena.

13. **(d)** Raju is just after Garima.

14. **(c)**

Left   A B C Ⓓ E F G H I J   Right

7th from the right

15. **(d)** Inner figure becomes outer and outer figure becomes inner and inner figure gets dots.

16. **(a)** One horse has 4 legs

As, 4 + 4 = 8

So, two horses have 8 legs.

17. (b) There are 10 + 10 + 3 = 23 fish in the box.

18. (d)

🎂	B$_1$	B$_2$	B$_3$	B$_4$	B$_5$	B$_6$
						B$_7$
						🐭

A mouse has to run 7 number of blocks to reach the cake.
Blocks (B1, B2, B3, B4, B5, B6, B7) = 7

19. (c) Brick is the heaviest item.

20. (b) Three such shapes are needed to form a circle.

21. (c)

SS$_1$	SS$_2$	SS$_3$
SS$_4$		SS$_5$
SS$_6$		SS$_7$
SS$_8$	SS$_9$	SS$_{10}$

Small Squares (SS1, SS2, SS3, SS4, SS5, SS6, SS7, SS8, SS9, SS10) = 10

22. (c) First figure of left pair is divided in two parts in second figure.

23. (b)

24. (d)

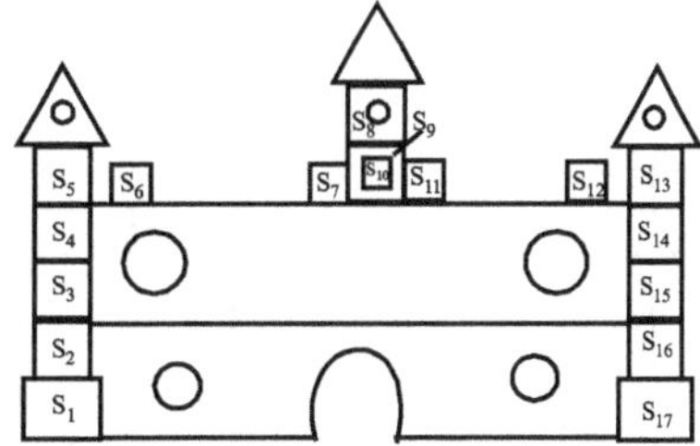

25. (b)  is heavier than [doll] and [dinosaur] is heavier than [doll] .

Order from the heaviest to the lighter is

26. (d) Elements in (a), (b) and (c) are all plane shapes.

27. (c) Mukul and Raghav do not like to eat grapes, so Aryan likes to eat grapes.

28. (c)

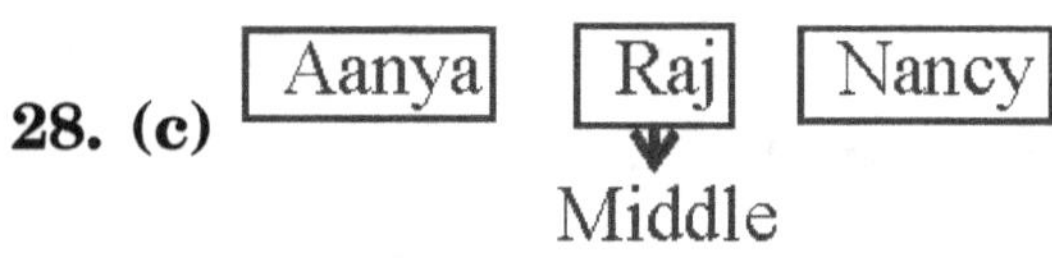

29. (c)

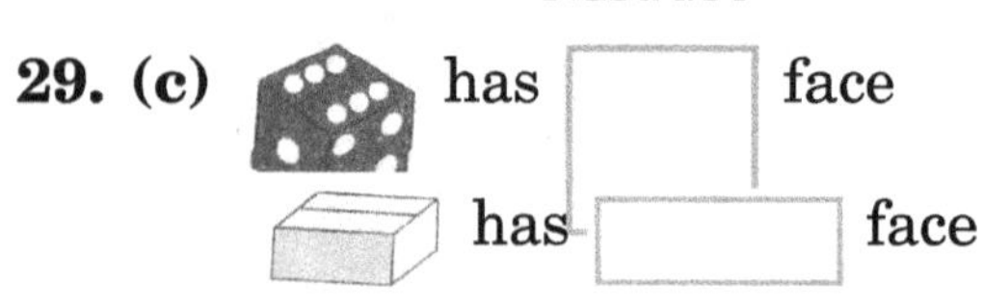

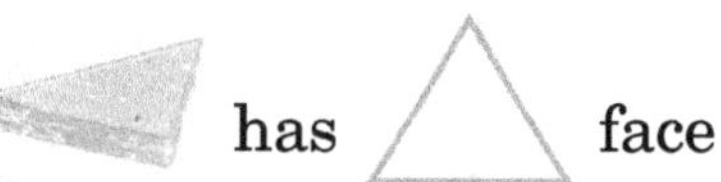

30. (b) Total children = 10

Number of girls = 6

Number of boys = $10 - 6 = 4$

MOCK TEST 3

ANSWER KEY

1	(d)	7	(a)	13	(a)	19	(d)	25	(d)
2	(b)	8	(b)	14	(a)	20	(a)	26	(b)
3	(b)	9	(a)	15	(d)	21	(d)	27	(c)
4	(c)	10	(d)	16	(c)	22	(a)	28	(c)
5	(a)	11	(d)	17	(c)	23	(a)	29	(b)
6	(c)	12	(b)	18	(b)	24	(c)	30	(a)

1. (c)

2. (b) Rule : Observe terms column-wise. Sum of first two terms is equal to the third term.

3. (b) S is the tallest and R is the shortest.

4. (c) In the given Figure 🍎 is lighter than 🍌 and 🍌 is lighter than 🍉

Order from the heaviest to the lightest : 🍉 🍌 🍎

5. (a) (6-8) N/L

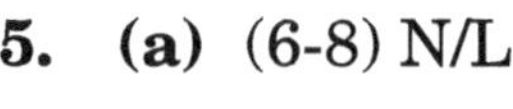

6. (c) Triangles (T_1, T_2, T_3, T_4, T_5, T_6, T_7, T_8) = 8

7. (a) Squares (S_1, S_2) = 2

8. (b) Circles = 6, Triangles = 8

9. (a) Elements in (b), (c) and (d) are three in number.

10. (d)

11. (d) Elements in (a), (b) and (c) are divided in two similar shapes.

12. (b)

13. (a)

14. (a) 4

15. (d) 

16. (c) 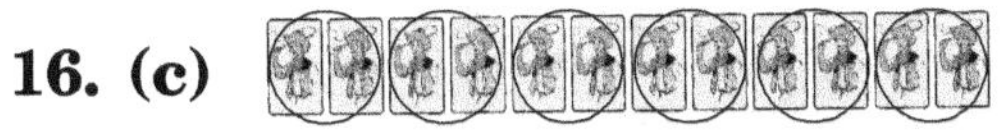

17. (c) 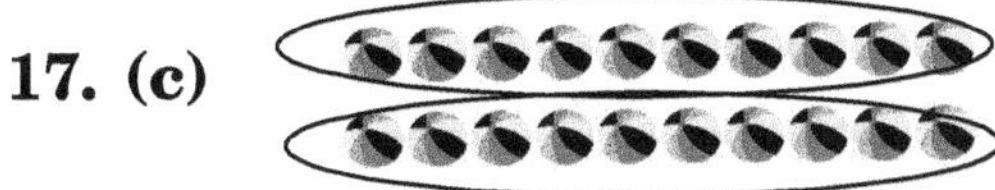

18. (b) Left pair is used together in a game.

19. (c) Number of line segments used to form first figure of the left pair is kept separately in second figure.

20. (a) Both are complementary pair.

21. (d)

22. (a)

23. (a) 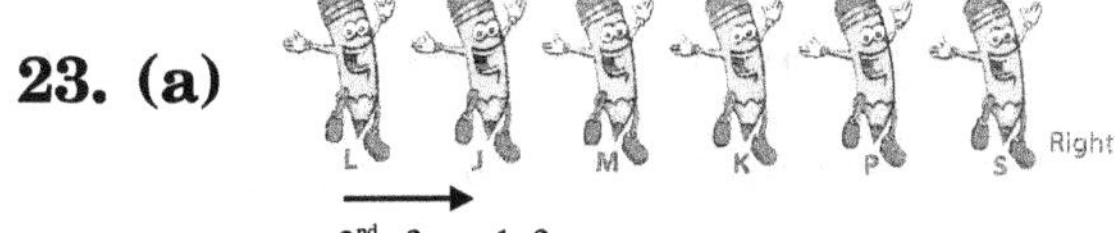

24. (c) 

Cubes $(C_1, C_2, C_3, C_4, C_5, C_6) = 6$

25. (d) 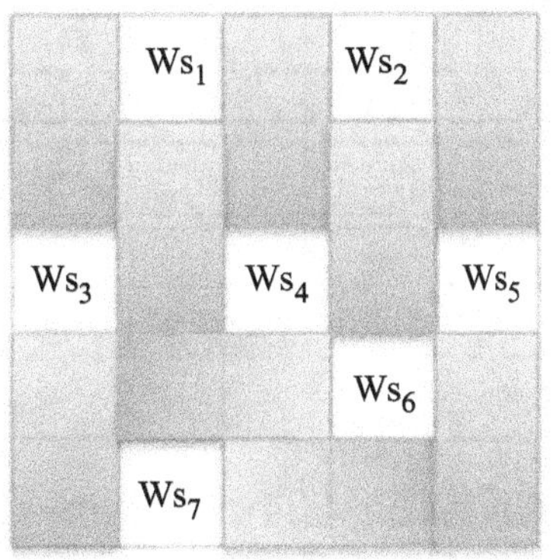

White Squares $(WS_1, WS_2, WS_3, WS_4, WS_5, WS_6, WS_7) = 7$.

26. (b) 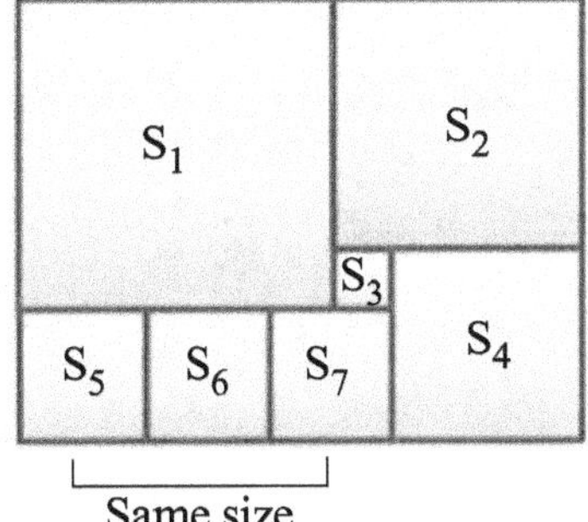

Square 5, Square 6 and Squre 7 are of the same size.

27. (c) The shape of ball is looking like a sphere.

(28 and 29):

Cat B > Cat A > Cat C

28. (c) Cat C is the youngest.

29. (b) Cat B is the oldest.

30. (a) Number 6 is in the middle.

MOCK TEST 4

ANSWER KEY									
1	(d)	7	(c)	13	(a)	19	(c)	25	(a)
2	(a)	8	(b)	14	(a)	20	(b)	26	(a)
3	(c)	9	(a)	15	(a)	21	(d)	27	(a)
4	(d)	10	(d)	16	(c)	22	(b)	28	(d)
5	(c)	11	(a)	17	(a)	23	(d)	29	(c)
6	(c)	12	(d)	18	(b)	24	(a)	30	(c)

1. (d) Each figure repeats itself after two figures.

2. (a)

$$22 \quad \textcircled{33} \quad 44 \quad 55 \quad 66$$
$$+11 \quad +11 \quad +11 \quad +11$$

3. (c) Difference between the numbers is 2.

$$20 \quad 18 \quad \textcircled{16} \quad 14 \quad 12$$
$$-2 \quad -2 \quad -2 \quad -2$$

4. (d) Two toy clowns = 18 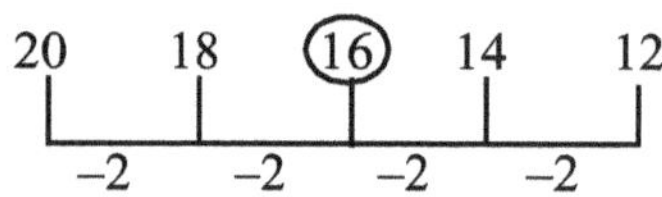. Hence, one toy clown = 9 .

5. (c) Weight if 1 Ⓟ ball = weight of 2 Ⓠ ball ⇒ Ⓟ is heavier than 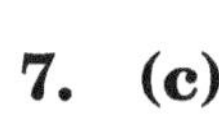 Ⓠ

Ⓠ is heavier than Ⓡ

Order from lightest to heaviest:

Ⓡ, Ⓠ, Ⓟ

6. (c)

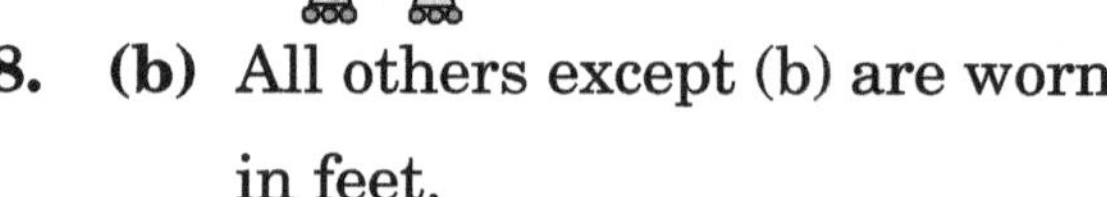

7. (c)

8. (b) All others except (b) are worn in feet.

9. (a) Elements in (b), (c) and (d) are used in winter season.

10. (d) 8 apples are on the tree.

11. (a) 4 apples are under the tree.

12. (d) 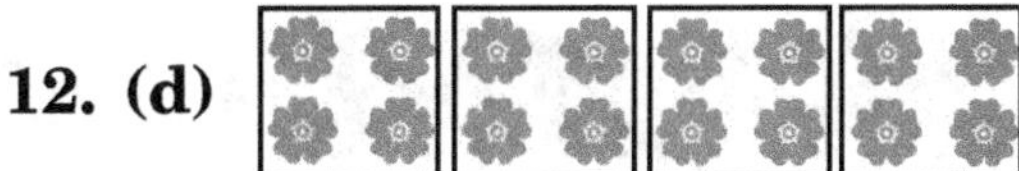

13. (a) 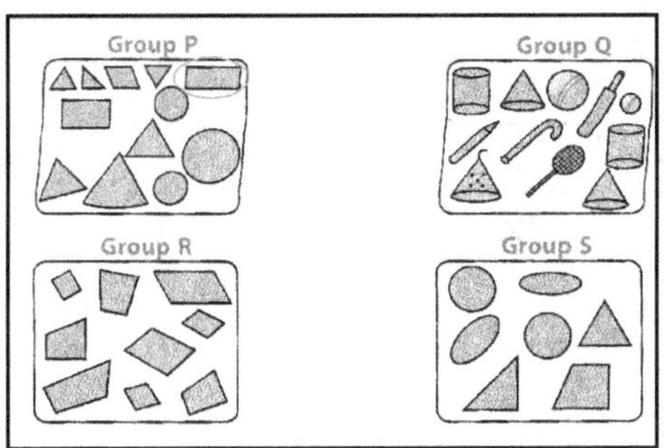 belong to group P only.

14. (a) Division of first figure is removed to make it whole figure.

15. (a) First figure can be put in the second figure in left pair.

16. (c) Second figure is reflection of first figure in left pair.

17. (a) The position of the flower in the circle is 3rd from the left end.

18. (b) Penguin T is in the first position.

19. (c) 3rd number from left = 9

Ist number from left = 17

Difference = 17 − 9 = 8

8 is the 2nd number from the right end.

(20-21) 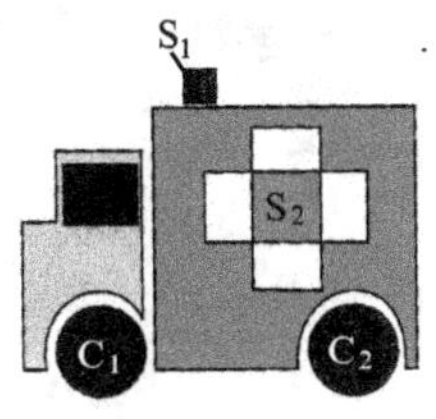

20. (b) Squares (S_1, S_2) = 2

21. (d) Circles (C_1, C_2) = 2

22. (b) Elements in (a), (c) and (d) are used by doctors only.

23. (d) Brick S is thickest.

24. (a) Brick P is thinnest.

(25 – 26)

Children	Pets
Rohan	Dog
Ankur	Bird
Pinki	Fish

25. (a) Rohan's pet is dog.

26. (a) Bird is Ankur's pet.

27. (a) Shape A has 3 sides.

28. (d) Shivam has 6 − 4 = 2 coins

29. (c) Total visible cubes = 5

To make a tower of 8 cubes

We need = 8 − 5 = 3 cubes.

30. (a)

MOCK TEST 5

ANSWER KEY									
1	(d)	7	(d)	13	(a)	19	(c)	25	(b)
2	(b)	8	(b)	14	(c)	20	(b)	26	(b)
3	(d)	9	(d)	15	(d)	21	(c)	27	(b)
4	(d)	10	(a)	16	(a)	22	(c)	28	(a)
5	(b)	11	(b)	17	(b)	23	(b)	29	(c)
6	(b)	12	(c)	18	(a)	24	(a)	30	(c)

1. **(d)** 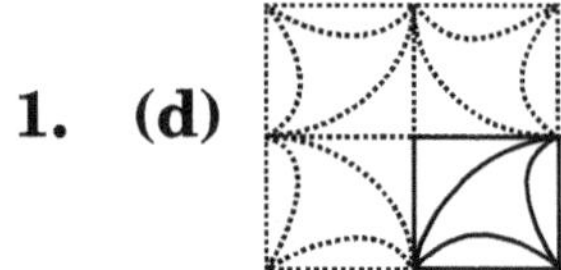

2. **(b)** Each design repeats itself after three designs.

3. **(d)**

$$3 \quad 6 \quad 9 \quad \boxed{12} \quad 15 \quad \boxed{18}$$
$$+3 \quad +3 \quad +3 \quad +3 \quad +3$$

4. **(d)** A is heavier than B or B is lighter than A

   C is heavier than B or B is lighter than C.

   Hence, A and C are heavier than B.

5. **(b)** Tomorrow is next day from today.

Today	Tomorrow
Sunday	Monday

6. **(b)** Length of stick P = 8 units

   Length of stick Q = 6 units

7. **(c)** Triangles = 6, Circles = 13

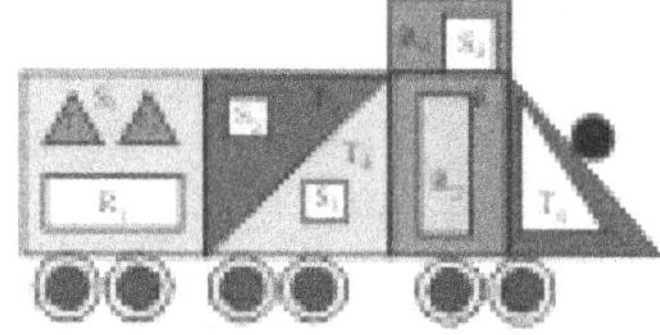

8. **(b)** Squares (S_1, S_2, S_3, S_4 and S_5) = 5

9. **(d)** Elements in (a), (b) and (c) are eatables.

10. **(a)** Elements in (b), (c) and (d) are road transport.

11. **(b)** 4 students are outside the school bus.

12. **(c)** 3 person are inside the school bus

13. **(a)** 3 planes are flying above the clouds.

14. **(c)** 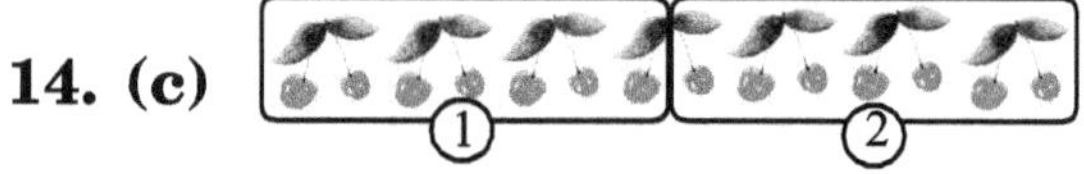

15. **(d)** Number of elements in left pair is increased by two from the first figure to the second

figure.

16. (a) Left pair belongs to the category of same transport.

17. (b) 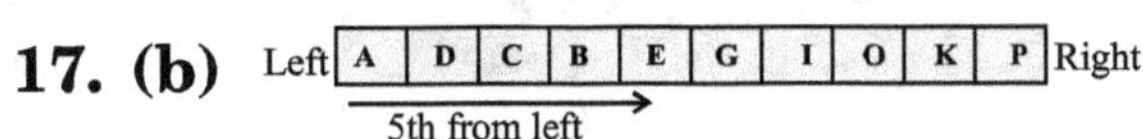

18. (a) 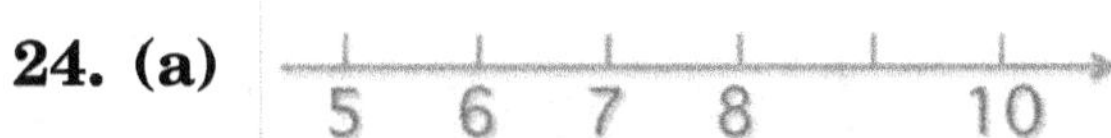

(19 & 20):

Birth order :

Mayank > Anshul > Shubam

19. (c) Shubam is the youngest.

20. (b) Mayank is the oldest.

21. (c) Number of Apples Neeraj has = 4

Number of Apples Sunny has = 4 – 1 = 3

22. (c) There are 3 + 2 + 2 = 7 windows.

23. (b) There are 7 stars inside the circle.

24. (a) 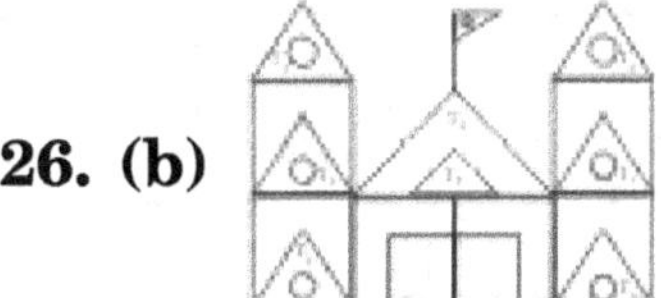

25. (a) There are 11 straight lines.

26. (b) 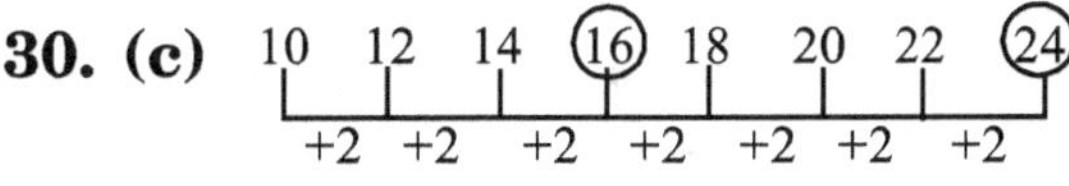

27. (b) Elements in (a), (c) and (d) are the birds.

28. (a) Inner element and outer element interchanges in left pair.

29. (c) Length of brush = 6 units

Length of pencil = 10 units

30. (c) 10   12   14   (16)   18   20   22   (24)

    +2   +2   +2   +2   +2   +2   +2

CYBER

MOCK TEST 1

<table>
<tr><td colspan="10" align="center">ANSWER KEY</td></tr>
<tr><td>1</td><td>(d)</td><td>6</td><td>(a)</td><td>11</td><td>(c)</td><td>16</td><td>(d)</td><td>21</td><td>(b)</td></tr>
<tr><td>2</td><td>(a)</td><td>7</td><td>(c)</td><td>12</td><td>(a)</td><td>17</td><td>(d)</td><td>22</td><td>(c)</td></tr>
<tr><td>3</td><td>(b)</td><td>8</td><td>(d)</td><td>13</td><td>(b)</td><td>18</td><td>(c)</td><td>23</td><td>(a)</td></tr>
<tr><td>4</td><td>(c)</td><td>9</td><td>(c)</td><td>14</td><td>(a)</td><td>19</td><td>(d)</td><td>24</td><td>(d)</td></tr>
<tr><td>5</td><td>(a)</td><td>10</td><td>(a)</td><td>15</td><td>(b)</td><td>20</td><td>(c)</td><td>25</td><td>(d)</td></tr>
</table>

1. (d) Palmtop, laptop and desktop are the types of computer but Tabtop is not a type of computer.

2. (a) In the given options a computer only can play music for you.

3. (b) i-3, ii-4, iii-2, iv-1

4. (c) We can take copy information from the computer screen on a sheet of paper (hardcopy) with the help of printer.

5. (a) Microwave is not a part of computer, it is a kitchen appliance.

6. (a) Mouse is used to point and select items on computer.

7. (c) In the given options, we can do weather forecasting and search for information by the help of computer.

8. (d) All of these

9. (c) While travelling we can use laptop and tablet, because these are small in size and can be easily carried.

10. (a) Monitor

11. (c) CapsLock

12. (a) Spacebar

13. (b) Clicking

14. (a) Mouse

15. (b) The wheel in center, shown in the given image of mouse is scroll wheel.

16. (d) Switch on the main power button.

17. (d) After the main power is on, we press the power button on UPS then we press the power button on CPU, at last switch on the monitor.

18. (c) The power button available on the laptop.

19. (d)

20. (c) It is used to fill the shapes with color and it cannot be used to draw shapes.

21. (b) It is used to fill the shapes with color

22. (c) Touch-screen

23. (a) App is an application program found in the Smartphone.

24. (d) 

25. (d) They all are wearable computers.

MOCK TEST 2

ANSWER KEY									
1	(b)	6	(d)	11	(a)	16	(a)	21	(b)
2	(d)	7	(d)	12	(c)	17	(d)	22	(d)
3	(d)	8	(d)	13	(c)	18	(c)	23	(d)
4	(c)	9	(a)	14	(a)	19	(a)	24	(d)
5	(b)	10	(b)	15	(d)	20	(a)	25	(d)

1. (b) Computer is an electronic machine and it is very fast man made machine.

2. (d) All of these

3. (d) 

4. (c) A central processing unit (CPU) is the electronic circuitry within a computer that carries out the instructions of a computer program by performing the basic arithmetic, logical, input/output (I/O) operations and control the overall working of computer.

5. (b) 

6. (d)

7. (d) All of these

8. (d) All of these

9. (a) Store information about students

10. (b)

11. (a) Keyboard

12. (c) Space bar

13. (c) Wireless means without a wire (cable).

14. (a) i-2, ii-3, iii-4, iv-1

15. (d) All of these

16. (a) Desktop

17. (d) Both a and b

18. (c) An uninterruptible power supply (UPS) is a device that allows a computer to keep running for at least a short time when the primary power source is lost. It also provides protection from power surges.

19.(a) 

20.(a) Ribbon area

21.(b)

22.(d) App is an abbreviated form of the word "application". An application is a software program that's designed to perform a specific task on mobile.

23.(d) All of these.

24.(d) All of these

25.(d) Smart-watch

MOCK TEST 3

ANSWER KEY									
1	(d)	**6**	(a)	**11**	(d)	**16**	(b)	**21**	(d)
2	(d)	**7**	(d)	**12**	(b)	**17**	(b)	**22**	(d)
3	(c)	**8**	(d)	**13**	(d)	**18**	(d)	**23**	(a)
4	(a)	**9**	(d)	**14**	(c)	**19**	(b)	**24**	(c)
5	(a)	**10**	(d)	**15**	(a)	**20**	(d)	**25**	(b)

3. (c) A central processing unit (CPU) is the electronic circuitry within a computer that carries out the instructions of a computer program by performing the basic arithmetic, logical, control and input/output (I/O) operations specified by the instructions. It is also known as brain of computer.

7. (d) A speaker is used for listening songs on computer.

8. (d) We use pencil and paper to draw paint on a computer.

9. (d) All of these.
Explanation: If we click the right button on the mouse then a list of commands display on the screen of computer. These commands can be used according to the requirement.

18.(d) Restart is a process of making computers shutdown safely and then starts it again.

19.(b) Booting is a process of powering on the computer and starting the operating system. The operating system is the program that makes all your software applications and hardware work together, and then everything is ready for use.

21.(d). The given figure is color tools in which we can choose the color and fill up the shapes or picture according to the requirement.

24.(c) A line tool, is used to draw straight lines of different thickness, color and length in ms-paint.